D1445244

415
T3

305, 8 D

A Safe Place to Talk

ABOUT RACE

10 Thought-Provoking Interviews with **Sharon E. Davis** from her *VoiceAmerica* radio show, "A Safe Place to Talk About Race."

Published by Healing Humankind LLC

Published by Healing Humankind LLC
For more information or requests for permission, visit
www.safeplaceonrace.com or call 888.569.5575

Cover, interior design and layout by Fortitude Graphic Design and Printing
Edited by Sonya Bernard-Hollins/Season Press LLC
Cover photo by John Grap

ISBN-13: 978-1-49484-649-7
ISBN-10: 1-49484-649-7

1. Racial Healing. 2. Diversity. 3. Sexual Preference 4. Discrimination
5. Race. 6. Civil Rights 7. Historical Racism 8. Racial Reconciliation
9. Racism 10. LGBT 11. Inclusion 12. Conflict Resolution 13. Social Justice

Printed in the United States of America
10 9 8 7 6 5 4 3 2 1

*This book is based on original interviews
from A *Safe Place to Talk About Race* radio show hosted
by Sharon E. Davis and have been slightly edited for print.

*White, Black and People of Color as it relates to a human being or group identity, and the
Civil Rights Movement as it relates to the African-American movement for equal rights from
the 1950s-70s, have been capitalized by decision of the author.

Dedication

To my loving parents, Herbert Peter and Jessie Belle Davis
and future generations of children who deserve more from us.

A Safe Place to Talk ABOUT RACE

Sharon E. Davis

CONTENTS

ACKNOWLEDGEMENTS

The number of people who have made *A Safe Place to Talk About Race* radio show and book possible are too numerous to list. I'd like to express my deepest love and regard to you as ardent listeners, and the many of you who pushed the envelope to make this a better experience by challenging and asking important questions and offering points of view that expanded the dialogue. Thank you for participating across the nation with calls, emails and text messages.

At the time of this book edition, each one of the 25 interview guests was "book worthy." I'm sorry it wasn't possible to include them all. We now have more than 50 guest interviews and we'll have a new problem to solve! Thank each and every one of my guests for the wisdom and brilliance you shared.

I've very grateful that Sterling Speirn found time in his busy schedule to pen the foreword to this book. He offered an invitation to engage in racial healing I rarely see in executive leadership. Thank you, Sterling.

The behind-the-scenes professionals: Leah Hubbard, guest coordinator from Wise Administrative Associates; Shirley Lund, information technology and web master from Lund and Lund; and John Amara Walters, student social media expert; you all kept me on track. Thank you all one thousand times!

The Kitchen Cabinet of friends and critical supporters kept me balanced and humble. They are alphabetically: Charles Bailey, Dr. Gail Christopher, Dr. James M. Croteau, Dr. Richard Davis, Scott Durham, Bonnie Fields Solas, Sharonne Fogle, Dr. Jeanne Gazel, Dr. Mary Hall-Thiam, David J. Hearndon, Pamela Johnson, Robert K. Johnson, Jr., Ronald L. Johnson, Cordelia Masterson, Clarence Aziz Mustafa-Sun Bey Masterson, Cindy Orlandi and J.R. Reynolds. And last, but not least, Joe and Clara Stewart for the strategic thinking, wisdom and ongoing commitment to racial healing.

FOREWORD

Sharon Davis and her guests have given us a wonderful gift: *A Safe Place to Talk About Race*. The ten interviewees she shares with us in this anthology bring perspectives and experiences as fresh and diverse as the variety of their backgrounds and their racial, ethnic and personal identities.

Although many of the individuals profiled here are experts and long-time practitioners – among them professors, a physician and a big-city mayor – what connects them all is a life-long passion for racial healing and a commitment to the hard work of not just talking about race, but to *do* race work in schools, in communities, in governments, in organizations, and in life.

Readers will have a unique experience of joining in the conversations Sharon conducted with her guests in heart-to-heart interviews on the radio. And they will find it easy to identify with the listeners who called in with many of the questions we would all want to ask, if only we had a 'safe place.'

As former Executive Director of the National Resource Center for the Healing of Racism, Sharon Davis is especially qualified to host this remarkable series of interviews. She is among a growing number of veteran practitioners who have devoted much of their careers to the cause of racial healing. When the W. K. Kellogg Foundation launched its unprecedented initiative *America Healing* (2010), our goal was to find partners, people and organizations to support as allies devoted to promoting racial healing, and to addressing and ultimately dismantling the legacy and structures of racism that continue to deny equal opportunities to far too many children and individuals in our society today.

Sharon's work at the National Center exemplified the hundreds of similar efforts we discovered throughout the United States. We wanted to invest in people and organizations working to inform and change hearts, minds and the deeply-held, often unconscious biases that are frequently at the core of structural racism. And now this anthology brings a fresh catalogue of voices and lives of inspiring dedication to welcome a whole new generation of allies across gender, race, ethnicity and sexual orientation to the crucial work of realizing the American Dream of opportunity and collective action.

Fundamental for all of us is to create safe places to talk about race, not limited to workshops or special events, but as the new normal, at home, at work, at houses of worship, on television and on the radio. I invite readers of these conversations to pull up a chair, make a list of the questions and issues and experiences you would like to discuss. And then roll up your sleeves to create many more safe places to talk about race, to talk about differences, and to discover through deep dialogue the oneness of humankind.

Sterling K. Speirn, *former President and CEO*
W. K. Kellogg Foundation

INTRODUCTION

IT'S PERSONAL

I remember the first time I realized that what my mind said I believed about races of people was not what I was feeling in the emotions of my heart. Realizing the distance between what I thought and how I felt, is where my racial healing began. It's very personal.

Racial healing is the personal and organizational work needed to restore the basic truth that we, as humans, came from the same source and are connected and dependent on one another physically, emotionally, socially, intellectually, and spiritually, forever. Simply put, the Oneness of Humankind is the fundamental basis of our species.

Racism has not always been part of human history (Richard Thomas, Ph.D., *Racial Unity: An Imperative for Social Progress, Detroit, Race and Uneven Development (Comparative American Cities)*. The world had practiced human slavery but not relegated human beings to beasts of the field or sub-humans. We further lost our way around 1400 AD and at the beginning of the Industrial Revolution. We started to come out of the BIG ditch (global enslavement of 'races' at a bestial level) around the 1840s.

Racial healing has a different mission and focus than Diversity-Inclusion. Both will be needed for a very long time. Racial healing addresses the emotional-if not spiritual-content of racism. The underpinning of racial healing is very much like Alcoholics Anonymous; it deals with finding out the facts and misinformation learned that shape a person's thoughts, actions, reactions, and world view.

IT'S A DIALOGUE

Dialogue is an essential element in the healing process. Why dialogue? It's not built on the foundation of debate. Dialogue allows people to get into a deeper and closer sharing of thoughts and feelings that only members of our human family can have. It is often harder for people with culturally European-trained backgrounds to engage in this mode of interaction. A central part of Western European education centers around asking questions to gain understanding, or to set things to the "left" or "right." The common communication mode is founded on debate. People of Color around the world generally grew up with dialogue.

Think of Native American tribal councils that listen to all points of view. That style of communication took precedence over contesting comments in a back-and-forth, point-by-point yes or no, fashion. Dialogue is sharing the secrets of our heart in a way that helps us reflect, discover and uncover the multiple facets of a topic by the group. It allows learning together about true feelings and perspectives. Dialogue is intimate. Debate, by design, fosters win/lose results. Both dialogue and debate are needed in the world. Dialogue, however, is essential for racial healing.

Racial healing shares some fundamentals of Alcoholics Anonymous. Yes. A human being starts with the spirit of someone greater than the human ego. We re-evaluate what we thinks we know. However, the truth– when clarified–grounds the subject to a new way of life. That new way of life includes more people with similar issues in recovery. And for most, it takes constant vigilance. Racial conditioning is so deep that even facilitators, writers, and interviewers of the topic can often get drawn back into preconceived racial patterns of thinking and behaving.

PREFACE

Racial Healing generally has the following primary elements or cycle:

1. **Conditioning:** Misinformation about humans who look differently. That is learned from someone you know, love, and trust, and is sometimes sealed for life. Constant reinforcement by family, friends, segregation, media, institutions, and sometimes experiences, may still linger today in our subconscious thoughts, unaware feelings, and actions. Conditioning happens to ALL cultures and races.

2. **Privilege:** When well-meaning people don't know how they are affected and don't see racial patterns, life seems normal in the smog of racism.

3. **Self Hate:** When People of Color believe the lie or misinformation about their group. This may lead to actions against self or one another.

4. **Institutional Barriers:** When companies, organizations, clubs and public policies are designed to exclude People of Color in some way.

5. **Common Species:** The Oneness of Humankind replaces racial sub-species categories and belief systems.

6. **Ally Building:** Learning how to support each other on the journey and continue to re-evaluate thoughts, views, and feelings about our human family.

There is no pill for racial healing. It is not usually an individual journey, and requires authentic learning assistance from each other.

WHY THIS BOOK? WHY NOW?

The objectives and goals of this book are to break through the noise and fear of the subject in order to learn, grow, and get better. There are luminaries in the world who have important things to say about the healing of racism that must come to light. Some of them are featured in this collection of interviews. They include parts of the puzzle that, when gathered together, help connect the dots for us all. Luminaries sometimes don't even know how important their contributions are on the healing of racism for the country and the world. It's hard, worrisome work that can take anyone to the emotional edge of insanity.

Racism changes its form as progress is made. We have discovered that through our conversations on our radio show, *A Safe Place to Talk About Race*. We take the best thinking and understanding from our experts and get the information out to the masses–the country and the world. We have a way to focus on THE biggest elephant in the room of America–racism. Our guests are committed to add to the continued rise of "We the People."

Like the ancient pyramids that can be seen from outer space, racial healing is built one giant stone at a time. It's important to capture the building process so that we never slip back. And, so that all can understand each stone and the contributions it makes for all of us. Luminaries have more to offer than what this book can contain. I've been privileged to know them and I hope you will seek them out through their contact information at the end of this book. Lastly, I encourage you to find your voice and add to the building and reclaiming of our entire human family any way you lovingly can.

WHAT CAN YOU EXPECT FOR YOUR TIME SPENT?

This book offers an invaluable support system to hold your hand through the highs and lows of racial healing. It gives you a way to seek solid information, sort out feelings based on misinformation (some would say, lies) and get on a new path towards a future that nourishes and rewards your personage for the betterment of you, your work, your children, and the world.

Through this book, I hope you will discover what you need to learn, and how to increase your ability to analyze, think, feel, and gain a thoughtful point of view about yesterday, today, and tomorrow. It should fill in many blanks to such questions as: *How we got here? What drives racism? How do we get out?* And, *What are some expected outcomes?*

What this book cannot do for you is supply answers to *all* your questions on race. Nor can it eliminate the angst you may feel at times. All races/cultures have important things to learn and unlearn. There is enough for each to do without trying to manage or lead other groups through their work. Why? Because each story is a long thread of lived experiences that only *that* group can untangle. And, trying to resolve some other person's pain may not leave energy to resolve your own. Think of yourself more as contributing your part.

WAYS TO BEST USE THIS BOOK

Independently: Read a chapter, answer the questions at the end, and begin to write your private racial healing journal. Write what you are discovering, thinking, feeling, and doing to revisit what racial issues you may have. Be sure to include your hopes and dreams for change, and your role in making it happen.

Classroom: Follow the direction of your instructor by reading the interviews, listening to the full interviews on your MP3, and discussing the topics. Use what you've learned toward future class assignments based on this book.

Book Club: Join or start a Racial Healing Dialogue group. Seek out others in your community for a reading and discussion session that will foster the "safe" atmosphere of honest, authentic discussion.

With each of these options, feel free to listen to the full chapter interviews available online at *A Safe Place to Talk about Race.* Take time to explore the web site, www.safeplaceonrace.com, reference books, articles, and other information about the radio guests.

Interview 1

Life After Hate:

A Former Skinhead Shares a Tale of

Racism and Redemption

My mom always told me that I could do anything in my life, and she would always support me, and would always love me. But, I was never to bring home someone Black or a woman (as a relationship) because that was grounds for pretty much excommunication from the family.

Angela King, former member of the Skinhead White Supremacists

ANGELA KING

Angela King is an educator, speaker, and consultant. She has earned recognition for her work in Prejudice Reduction and Holocaust education.

She was a panelist at the 2011 Google Summit Against Violent Extremism, in Dublin, Ireland, and at a 9/11 commemoration on terrorism held in Washington D.C. She is a correspondent and character educator for LifeAfterHate.org and is currently writing a memoir.

THE DIALOGUE

Angela King was the first guest on our show, *A Safe Place to Talk About Race*, which aired in June 4, 2012 on *VoiceAmerica* internet radio. She is a courageous young women who was willing to share her personal story about how the most overt types of racism can grab our vulnerable children. In her story of finding out the truth about our human family and escaping the snare of violence, she has become a wonderful role model for us all.

King grew up in South Florida where messages from her church and family led to her confusion about race and sexuality. She then gravitated toward those who shared the same racist and homophobic beliefs on which she was raised. She became a Skinhead.

The radical White supremacist organization was founded in the United Kingdom and eventually adopted Neo-Nazi beliefs of hatred against non-Anglo-Saxons. Known for wearing bald or shortly cut hair and performing hate crimes, their methodology migrated into the United States during the 1980s, bringing with it White supremacist beliefs coupled with violent hate crimes against everyone from six-year-old Black children, to Jewish store owners.

Angela fell pray to the rhetoric and participated in a life of crime, which led her to prison. What she learned while incarcerated with women from various races and backgrounds, helped her break free from racial bigotry.

POINT 1
Where and How Racial Harm Begins?

SHARON: Angela, where did your beliefs on race come from?

ANGELA: I really felt that I was growing up in a normal way and in a normal place with normal beliefs, and I really wasn't. To an extent, both of my parents were prejudice and homophobic. They clung to what I think of as old-fashioned racism against certain groups–but not all groups–that were different from us.

I also grew up in a very rural area where there was literally no diversity. I went to a private school up until the age of 10 or 11. My parents were very strict on me and very rigid.

I started to develop almost an identity crisis where I struggled to fit in. I had no self-confidence at all. I felt very competitive and just started to feel like I didn't fit in anywhere.

The very first time I was physically bullied was the last time. I took on the role of the bully.

My parents told me things that, looking back now in retrospect, could have been told to me in a very different way. A good example; my mom always told me that I could do anything in my life, and she would always support me, and would always love me. But, I was never to bring home someone Black or a woman, as a relationship, because that was grounds for pretty much excommunication from the family. I grew up with that kind of mentality hanging over my head.

From this very early age, it was not just any old identity crisis. It was an acute identity crisis. Mix that with no self-esteem.

I was eventually bullied, and then became a bully, and set out on this horrible path of self-destruction.

It was not until I went into the sixth grade at a public school that I really started to be around other people who were different from me, either racially, religiously or culturally. And by that point I think I had developed somewhat of a fear, because I didn't know anything about other people. What I knew at home was all I really knew.

Actually, I think my further downward spiral was the first time I was physically bullied in the seventh grade. At that point, I guess I had so much anger and resentment built inside me from feeling like the misfit and learning what I learned at home, that the very first time I was physically bullied, was the last time. I took on the role of the bully.

For the next few years I literally just fought with every one and any one I came across. I started experimenting with drugs, alcohol, and sex. Mind you, I was at a very young age and doing things that even adults can't handle the repercussions of. I didn't realize that the more I did to act out the more I was damaging myself and my inner spirit.

POINT 2
When Misinformation Meets Opportunity

SHARON: *How were you approached to join a group like the skinheads?*

ANGELA: It was in high school that I met a group of kids that were also misfits. They went around wearing things or talking about things that begged attention. It started with anarchy symbols and just acting out, and eventually they came to school wearing swastikas.

When I started seeing what they were wearing, the one thing that I noticed the most was that they really seemed to command attention. They made people angry. At that young age, I mistook the fear and disgust for respect.

I thought, 'Wow, people respect them and get out of the way when they walk by.' It wasn't long after, that I found I was really finding a place to fit in. Around them, I could be angry, I could be violent, and I didn't have to explain it. I didn't have to talk about it.

I asked them for information and to introduce me to the older skinheads and racists they were getting their information from. The racism that I learned at home was almost like a springboard for me. I went in there and racism was something that I already knew. I used that to my advantage.

I said, 'Well, I already know about this group because my parents always told me about them,' and 'I have this racist flyer because I got it from my father.' It got me a little bit past the get-to-know-you, make-sure-you're-really-with-us stage. I loved being involved with them because I felt like I finally had a place where I belonged. It was like I found a family outside of my family.

I remained involved in, and a member of the racist underground for nearly a decade of my life. I was a member of several different violent groups that have been noticed around the country for committing hate violence.

There were times that I felt very briefly that I was doing something wrong and that I didn't want to live in that life any more. To be quite frank with you, once you're involved, you can't wake up one day and say, "I changed my mind. I don't want to do this anymore."

There was one point when I had tried to distance myself and woke up one morning with bullet holes in the building I lived in.

7

CALLER: Scott asks: *Angela, what an incredible story and thanks for having the courage to come on and share it with us. I'm a public school teacher and the thing that I think concerned me the most is that as you were growing up and displaying signs in the school, that there wasn't more interest put in you and your group by the other adults in your high school.*

I'm wondering, was there an attempt made by any teachers, administrators, or adults in your life, or if not, can you think of a way that teachers should be aware of these things? And maybe, what could they do to instead indoctrinate children in this concept of oneness rather than an indoctrination of hate?

ANGELA: In school, there was no intervention or attempt. I have to just throw in there that even though I was an adolescent, I'm the one who is completely responsible for the things that I did and the decisions I made. And yes, the adults in my life should have been there to intervene, but ultimately that burden lies with me.

Let me throw out an example to show the mentality of individuals in the school that I attended. I had a project in my earth science class to build a moon base. We were literally told build it like you would if you were really going to live in one. I was bored and I guess wanting to cause trouble, so I put a great big swastika on mine.

My instructor didn't say a word when I handed it in. I did not get reprimanded until over a week later when a student went home and complained to a parent. My punishment, wasn't a punishment. I got a "B" on my project and it was no longer displayed publicly with the other students' projects.

SHARON: *Angela, I don't know whether that says so much about you, as a young person. Quite frankly, you were just born into that story so it's not any blame on you, but what it says about the adults that thought that was absolutely okay. There's a lot of learning that needs to go on.*

CALLER: Pamela asks: *One of the key questions that I had was in terms of women in the skinhead groups that you participated in. How are women viewed? Did they ever really take on a leadership role themselves?*

ANGELA: Women are viewed very much as baby makers. We are told in the racist underground that the most constructive thing that we can do for our race and for the struggle that we claim we have, is to literally just propagate and continue having White children.

There's this mentality that the White race is going to be extinct. And that's how women are made to feel important and that they're needed and wanted.

POINT 3
The Violent Reality of Hate

It wasn't until I was in my early 20s that things started to spiral even more out of control. I started getting in trouble with the law from a very early age and it continued to spiral downward from there.

In my early 20s, I was involved in an armed robbery of a Jewish-owned store. I took part in this robbery with a handful of other racist skinheads. We targeted the location because we thought, or assumed, it would be owned or operated by someone who was not White.

During this robbery, I sat in the vehicle. I knew that a robbery was going to take place, that someone could be seriously harmed, even killed. And I did nothing to stop it. Because of my part in that crime I found myself –at the age of 23– in a federal correctional institution.

To be quite honest, when I first was incarcerated for that crime, I felt like I had no responsibility. I told myself, *All I did was sit in the car. How could I possibly be in trouble?*

Then a few different thoughts started to come to me. When I was brought there, I was put into solitary confinement. The prison officials didn't know if I was going to go into the population of other inmates and start problems or if someone would have a problem with me.

At about age 15, unfortunately, I started covering my body with tattoos -blatantly racist tattoos. So, I had about a month to sit in solitary confinement and think about why I was there.

When I started speaking to my appointed lawyer, I began really digesting what I had done. And I was scared. I went from abusing minorities to becoming a minority. And that was just a crash course for me; the very first part in completely changing my mentality and my life.

I was incarcerated with women from all over the world, from just about every nationality and religion one could think of. These were women that yes, they were criminals. They were in a correctional institution with me, but these were women that I never, in my entire life, would have even considered getting to know, having a conversation with, sharing any kind of stories or personal narratives. And on top of that, it was very much me feeling that well, I was a skinhead and there certainly aren't any other racists around me now. So, I truly was a minority in a couple of different senses.

SHARON: Does any particular incident come to mind when you were incarcerated and you maybe ate with a wider variety of people than you'd ever experienced in your life, and you said to yourself, "Uh-oh," or "I'm afraid," or "I want to get to know that person," or someone befriended you?

ANGELA: While sitting with a group of Jamaican women I had become friends with, one of them asked me, "Why were you racist? Why did you hate everybody? If you ever met me on the street, what would you have said or done? Would you beat me up?"

I tried to explain it, but at the time-and even now-I'm still trying to sort out the pieces of my life and trying to make sense of my decisions. And all of a sudden, in the middle of this conversation, she very matter-of-factly said, "I always hated White people."

I was blown away. I never thought that there could be racism except from where I learned it. She explained that where she was from in Jamaica she had very little contact with Caucasians. And the little contact she had was with individuals who went there on vacation and pretty much treated the natives like they were just there to serve them and their needs. That was her view of White people.

It was just an amazing experience to sit and talk so candidly and to get that kind of an understanding into ideas and experiences that I would never have on my own.

SHARON: This is extraordinary. And I know that it happens a lot that way. And it really brings home one of the foundational elements of why we do this show. We are all members of the same human family, and because we are, that means that any of us can think like a racist.

We learn this kind of thinking, and talking, and belief system, and we're working our way out of it. Yes, we're members of the same human family.

POINT 4
The Road to Redemption and Love

ANGELA: Upon my release, I was absolutely petrified. I wondered over and over, I cried. I was so worried that I had somehow hard-wired myself, my brain to always have a racist attitude and a racist mentality, and that I would never be able to shake those things.

Truly, it was almost like having to unlearn a bad habit. I have to be absolutely honest and say that there was a point in time when I would see someone of another race, and even though I wasn't still clinging to that hatred, I would automatically think a horrible name or some stereotypical thought. It literally took me stopping and trying to view them through a different lens and really try to analyze and ask myself, *Why did you think that? Is there a reason?* And it was in that way that I learned to break this horrible habit.

I think that one of the most important aspects of that is to be honest with ourselves and not just sweep those things under the rug and pretend that they don't exist. Because that's only going to hide them in a dark corner where they're going to fester and grow.

I was scared not only of the thought that I might not be able to break out of that mind set, but also because during my incarceration I came to the decision that I was going to cooperate fully with authorities. I ended up testifying against another racist.

I felt like I needed to make a stand, and making my break, I was going to do it in the right way, because it was the right thing to do. I hadn't done the right thing for so many years.

In 2001 when I was released, I went into college a few months later. I started speaking publicly. This was about eleven years ago now.

Over those past eleven years, I earned three degrees. I've made it to a Master's degree and have been accepted into a doctoral program. And quite honestly, I need a break. I just couldn't cram any more into my brain at that time.

I still need to understand a lot. Just because I'm not in school right now doesn't at all mean that I'm not actively learning about the world and what surrounds me. When I was in prison, I learned to take responsibility, and that changed my view of the world completely.

I also learned to love myself and not to put myself down. And, that it was okay to be different and not have to fit in with any groups as long as I loved who I was.

SHARON: At some point, Angela, did you feel that you might be afraid that someone might discover who you were before, not who you are now?

ANGELA: Not really. I am an open book. And to be honest, after spending three years in prison there isn't much that can embarrass me. And I think that's one of the things that has also guided me–honesty.

I have found that from the beginning, when I meet an individual or encounter other individuals or even organizations or companies, it's very important that I'm honest. From the time I was released from prison I have never tried to hide my past. Yes, I regret the person that I was. I feel this huge sense of guilt for the things I did and said and the ways that I hurt people. But, I also know that I would not be able to do what I do now if I did not have those experiences.

I would absolutely change what I did to hurt others, whether it was physically, mentally, emotionally, or spiritually. But I would never change the fact that I went to prison or that I had these experiences, because quite honestly, they helped. It helps to be able to share honestly and openly, and let other individuals know that there is hope.

SHARON: You now work with a group of individuals who want to bring attention to the destruction of hate. How did that come about?

ANGELA: I was invited to attend the Summit Against Violent Extremism in 2010, in Ireland. It was sponsored by Google Ideas, the Tribeca Film Festival, and the Council on Foreign Relations. They brought former members of violent extremist groups together with survivors of extremist violence, and other individuals from the private sector and governments.

I met this group of individuals and I learned, for probably the first time, that I am not alone. And, that there are other people who have been through very similar experiences. I met some individuals who were former skinheads and other formers from extremist groups. They founded the online magazine called, *Life After Hate.* It launched in 2010 on the Dr. King holiday.

When we met in Ireland, we were all so happy and so relieved to know that we weren't alone out there. We weren't alone in the experiences we had, and we made a commitment to one another to share our personal narratives, and to do so with compassion and with open, honest dialogue.

I was thrown this mix of horribly negative ingredients that was a recipe for disaster, and I have to say I'm appreciative that people call me courageous and tell me that I'm brave.

I'm just so proud to say that in January 2011, we got our nonprofit status. We have an online magazine that has seen over fifty authors from five continents, and we get hundreds and thousands of new visitors to our website monthly. We do so many great things. We do character outreach. We go out and really help with areas other than racism. We deal with bullying, gang violence, addiction, you name it. I'm also writing a memoir tentatively titled, *The Road I'm On: Life Inside and Out of the Racist Underground.*

I was thrown this mix of horribly negative ingredients that was a recipe for disaster, and I have to say, I'm appreciative that people call me courageous and tell me that I'm brave. I don't feel like I'm doing anything but making the right decisions, because for so many years, I didn't make the right decisions.

Interview Summary

Many keep asking why does racism persist? Won't it ever go away? Angela's story gets at the most profound level of racism. Any of us can be, and are racially conditioned with some of the most outlandish stories and experiences that color–yes, color our outlook. Our conditioning influences our beliefs, future experiences, and ability to grow into our full measure of what it really means to be human.

Racism is that slippery slope that any of us can travel. And we may not even realize we're falling into a ditch until something happens to help us realize where we are, and hopefully help us understand how we got out.

Points for Discussion

1) When did you first realize there were people different than you, or that you were different than another ethnic group?

2) Who or what influenced your thinking about different races, cultures, ethnic groups?

3) What fears do you have about other groups of people? Can you articulate them? Where did they come from?

Reader's Notes

_____
_____
_____
_____
_____
_____
_____
_____
_____
_____
_____
_____
_____
_____
_____

Interview 2

White Privilege:

Unraveling the White Privilege

Knot...not?

From the very beginnings of this country, before it was ever a country, the European settlements were run by a very small number of so called free White men. That's always been true. The country has always been organized to always be consistent with the interests of that group. Then you have everyone else.

Allan G. Johnson
Sociologist, Author

ALLAN G. JOHNSON

Allan G. Johnson is a public speaker, sociologist, nonfiction writer, and novelist who devotes his life to understanding the human condition. He has a particular focus on systems of privilege based on gender, race, and social class.

His social justice work focuses on what we can do to understand and change our shared legacy of life, organized around oppressive systems of privilege, power, and difference. Unraveling the knot of privilege begins with getting clear about what privilege really is, what it's got to do with each of us, and how everyone can see themselves as part of the process of change toward something better.

In his book, *Privilege, Power, and Difference*, he teaches us how to think critically about inequality and oppression without getting mired in guilt or despair. Then he shows us how to walk the talk, and turn our beliefs in justice and equality into practice. Oprah Winfrey's *O Magazine* named his first novel, *The First Thing and the Last*, as one of its "Great Reads" for April 2010.

THE DIALOGUE

Allan G. Johnson is a White, straight, male, who has spent thirty years doing deep personal work and thinking on many of the 'isms.' What does he see that's needed for the next breakthrough on race?

He has a perspective on race and class that offers a practical, compassionate, and readable guide to understanding what we're stuck in and how to search for a way out. But will it take deep pain, shameful remorse, and giving up any part of what many feel has been earned by a hard work ethic?

Yes, Johnson's social justice work focuses on our shared legacy. He says: *I did not invent the system of White privilege. It came into the world long before I did. I don't feel guilty because I was born as someone who's identified as White. That's not a reason for me to feel guilty. I am here now. We are all the ones who are participating in this system that we inherited, and however it's going to happen, we're the ones who are going to make it happen the way it happens. That means that even though I'm not to blame for this being the way it is, I have a profound responsibility for what's going to become of it.*

SHARON: Dr. Allan G. Johnson, what is White privilege really? Is it a myth or popular catch phrase that means a thousand things to a thousand people? It may spark more argument and barriers among races of people.

Some say it makes White people the new target. Is this one reason we find it harder to move forward on race matters as a country and around the globe? A knot is a powerful historical symbol in U.S. culture. It's made to hold and not easily let go.

POINT 1
Privilege is Social

ALLAN: A lot of people I find, think of the idea of privilege as simply meaning you have something that's good that other people *don't* have. For example, I'm taller than most people; that gives me an advantage as I can reach things up on a high shelf. So I have an advantage over shorter people. It has some of the characteristics of privilege in that it's an advantage I have, but didn't earn. I didn't do anything to become tall; it's an advantage that's exclusive to tall people.

Another characteristic that's required for something to be defined as privilege, is that it's not only something that's *unearned*, it's not only something that's *exclusive* to a particular group of people, but it's also something that is socially conferred.

> We will tend to think of human beings as being White, and People of Color as being something other than full human beings.

There's nothing about my being able to reach top shelves that requires people recognize me as tall, or see me as tall. It's just something I'm able to do. If you look at CEOs in the United States for example, and you compare their average height with the height of other people, they tend to be taller than average.

Then you look at research that shows that people tend to perceive tall people as having all kinds of valued attributes not attributed to shorter people. They're seen as being more intelligent and better leaders. All these characteristics have nothing to do, really, with how high you are off the ground.

Now we're talking about attributions that are made to people based on their height that give them advantages that they didn't earn. Now we're talking about privilege. As soon as you add that third element, that it's *socially conferred*, then you're talking about privilege.

SHARON: *Does a person know when he or she has been given the privilege by others? Does the person have to believe it?*

ALLAN: We're born and raised in a culture that's full of all kinds of images that provide us with a world view. And that world view is the lens that we look at everything with. If I think that tall people are better than short people, I've learned that; and I have learned that from my culture.

Of course the culture then gets mediated through all kinds of people. People who makes movies, parents, school teachers, and so on. There are all of these ways in which the content of a culture gets transmitted to us in one way or another. That becomes part of our world view.

As a recent study showed, they asked White people to close their eyes and picture a drug dealer. They gave them a minute to do that, and then they ask them to describe what they're seeing in their mind.

In the book, *The New Jim Crow* by Michelle Alexander, it states that 95% of those studied included in their descriptions that it was a Person of Color, even though 85% of the drug dealers in the United States are White.

POINT 2
Visual Images Seal the Deal

CALLER: Bob from Detroit, asks: *Do you think that Hollywood perpetuates the myth of White privilege based on White family story lines and does not do the same for African Americans?*

ALLAN: That's been part of our culture for as long as frankly there have been movies. In the *Information Please, Almanac* you can look up the films that win the Oscar each year for the Best Picture. I looked them up. Going all the way back to 1965, if you look at it in terms of race, there are basically no films, I mean zero, that have won the Oscar for Best Picture in which the story of the film is about a human being having human experiences, and the character just happens to be of Color.

If you look at the films that won Oscars where characters of Color are featured prominently, the films are invariably about race. *Crash* in 2005, for example. *Driving Miss Daisy*, 1989. *Gandh*i gets the Oscar because it's in India, and of course it's Gandhi. You've got to be Gandhi to get the Oscar here. Then you go back to 1967, all the way back to 1967, *In The Heat of the Night* with Sidney Poitier and Rod Steiger. The film is about race. The message here is that People of Color in films don't get to be featured in prominent roles unless the film is about race. They don't get to simply be human beings.

White people on the other hand, White characters and stories that are told through the perspectives of White people's lives, routinely portray them as simply human beings having various kinds of experiences. In 2011, it was, *The Artist*. The year before that, *The King's Speech*. In 2009, it was *The Hurt Locker*, where the main character is White. *The Hurt Locker* is not about him being White. *The King's Speech* is not about the King of England being White, it's about him being a man who has a speech difficulty and struggles to overcome it.

The Hurt Locker is about a man, a soldier, who has this terribly dangerous job and what his experience is doing it. It's not about his skin color. But, *In The Heat of the Night*, Sidney Poitier gets this incredible starring role, but it has to be about his race. He doesn't just get to be a Chicago police officer. That's the message that gets sent.

The default that comes out of that is we are constantly barraged with associations that say: Human being, White. Human being, White. Human being, White. Then we will tend to think of human beings as being White, and People of Color as being something other than full human beings. That's the implicit thing that comes out of that. And of course if you ask White people, "Do you think that People of Color are human beings?" Most people will say, "Of course they're human beings."

POINT 3
The Subconscious

These subconscious associations that we are presented with thousands and thousands of times in our lives, have very powerful effects on our unconscious associations. Which then can have all kinds of consequences for how we interact with other people; what we see as problematic. Whether when we picture a drug dealer do we tend to see people of a certain race? The answer is, Yes, we do. And we weren't born that way, we have been *taught* that.

CALLER: Pam from Michigan comments that: *Basically European Americans or White people don't understand that wealth continues to be built based on this White privilege; that Blacks will never get ahead. What's your reaction to that? Is this hopeless? Big question.*

ALLAN: Is it hopeless? Well, I think in the absence of some really large scale change, yeah, things are going to stay the way they are. They're going to get worse on a population level. Clearly individual People of Color can succeed. There are all kinds of examples of that, including the current president of the United States.

On a population level, the White advantage in the United States has just increased by a phenomenal amount in the last three or four years because of the way the financial meltdown affected People of Color differently than it affected White people. As of December 2009, everybody of course lost wealth as a result of the financial meltdown, and the median level of White wealth in White households dropped by 34%, down to $94,600. The median figure for Black households dropped by 77%.

That's just colossal. Whole generations of Latino and Black households lost generations of accumulated wealth, particularly in their houses. At the same time we might have individual Blacks who might be quite successful, as a population. And you can also of course have many individual Whites who are not particularly successful. As populations, the gulf between White people and everybody else has grown astronomically. Not simply because the White 1% has done so much better than everyone else, but because there's been such a devastating loss among People of Color.

POINT 4
Will White Privilege Ever End in the U.S.?

From the very beginnings of this country, before it was ever a country, the European settlements were run by a very small number of so called free White men. They weren't indentured servants, they weren't women, and so on. That's always been true. The country has always been organized to always be consistent with the interests of that group. Then you have everyone else. Then you have all the other White people in this country. To me the question is going to become, "What's going to happen to those two groups?" How are those two groups going to respond to this demographic change?

I'm pretty confident about how the elite is going to respond. They're going to have more and more gated communities. Their huge wealth is going to be used to protect their huge wealth. They're doing it already.

Then, the big question is going to be what about the rest of the White population who is struggling? The bottom 60%, the bottom 70% that is either struggling, has fallen below the poverty level, or they're living with tremendous insecurity. How are they going to respond to this situation?

Historically, that question has become the question of are they going to focus their attention on People of Color as the cause of their difficulty, or are they going to focus their attention on an economic system that allows such a small minority of people to have so much of the wealth? Are they going to focus on that as the problem?

I think what happens to us as a country and perhaps globally is going to depend on what happens in that moment. It's going to depend on where the weight falls in terms of how the world gets seen. One hundred years ago, the labor movement in the United States was tremendously powerful because they focused their attention on the capitalist system itself. They were not only powerful, but they accomplished some, for them, amazing things which we now take for granted.

A forty-hour work week, unemployment insurance, safe working places, all those safety regulations about factories and everything, those came from that era. Those who were in charge of the country fought tooth and nail against every single one of them. Getting rid of child labor, getting children out of factories, dangerous factories, was fought tooth and nail by the people who owned those factories and the politicians that represented their interests.

All of that came out of a labor movement, that focused on the economic system itself as problematic. Now they don't. Now those who are in power have managed to portray unions as so terrible that unions are vilified and everyone thinks unions are so terrible.

Now the question is, how are we going to respond to what's happening in this country economically and demographically? I don't know. I don't have a crystal ball. How we do respond is going to determine the future of this country. I think that conversations like this are important, because I want to add as much weight as I can in the direction of having a realistic view of what's actually happening, and what our choices really are.

White labor unions wouldn't admit People of Color for a long time. And then one time, the time came when it dawned on them that this was a dumb thing that they were doing, they started admitting People of Color. I don't know to what extent that decision was based on them realizing that keeping People of Color out was also the wrong thing to do. But, that shift in identification, of having class solidarity being more important than racial solidarity, that was critical one hundred years ago to successfully challenging the ruling class in terms of working conditions and all of that stuff.

I think we're at a similar moment of truth these days. I think the Occupy Wall Street movement was a wonderful thing. Because for the first time I think in my lifetime frankly, those kinds of questions were getting asked in public. They forced those questions, which are really about class, the class structure in this country, which is of course the source of racism. Racism came out of the capitalist industrial revolution. It was an economic phenomenon, first and foremost.

Forcing the issue to talk about class, which then of course brings in the phenomenon of race, I think is really important to do. I'm not suggesting that this is all about class and not about race, that race is not an issue, it's all class. That's not true at all. I think the reality is that you cannot separate race and class really, in this country. A big part of the payoff for being White, is better chances in terms of class.

POINT 5
White Male Reactions and Feelings

CALLER: *Juanita from California had a couple of questions related to what you found to be the most effective way to engage White middle class men and White working class men who may feel defensive or attacked* *when discussing these matters? What language or approach have you found to be full of pitfalls or less effective when communicating with these groups of men?*

ALLAN: I think the most important thing is to shift people's world view. That White men tend to go right to feeling defensive and feeling like they're being attacked, feeling like they're being picked on because they don't understand the concept of privilege as it's being used; they think it's all about them.

They don't understand how good people can participate in systems that produce terrible consequences. It's the normal state of things in our lives. Just because we're living in a society that is racist, that is organized in ways so that as most people go about their lives in the way they're expected to do it, produces terrible consequences. White men think that means they're terrible. It does not.

My goal is to shift people's point of view on our history and on our current situation, so that they can start to see the ways in which this is *not* about them. This is not about there being good people or bad people. This is about something much larger than that.

I think that's a liberating moment. I'm 60 years old. I did not invent the system of White privilege. It came into the world long before I did. I don't feel guilty because I was born as someone who's identified as White. That's not a reason for me to feel guilty. That isn't doing something. I am here now.

We are all the ones who are participating in this system that we inherited, and however it's going to happen, we're the ones who are going to make it happen the way it happens. That means that even though I'm not to blame for this being the way it is, I have a profound responsibility for what's going to become of it.

It's that shift from guilt-which I think is useless-to responsibility, that makes all the difference in the world. Because this is our society, this is our world, we're the ones who are alive, we're the adults. That means that we own this. This belongs to us.

None of us today have fought in the American Revolution. We are not responsible for the Declaration of Independence or the Constitution. We didn't do any of those wonderful things, and yet we somehow feel it's okay for us to feel proud of those things.

My belief, is that morally, we don't get to pick and choose. We don't just get to say, "Well I'm just going to own the things that I feel good about in the history of this country that I had nothing to do with. The things that I don't feel proud of that I also had nothing to do with, I'm going to just disown those." If we are Americans, that means we are the inheritors of the whole thing, the entire legacy. The good things and the horrible things.

My message to White people is we have to get over this being about us so that we can see the ways in which it is profoundly about us. It's not about us being good or bad. It's not about us being made to feel guilty. It's about us stepping forward as true citizens, as true adults, to take our share of responsibility for what needs to be done with something that is not simply a matter of history but is alive and well still.

The consequences are playing out every single day in this country. The consequences go all the way back to the institution of slavery, all the way back to the genocide and ethnic cleansing that were inflicted on Native Americans. That legacy is not just history. It is continuing to play out in real and material ways today, on Indian reservations, in ghettos, in the criminal justice system, everywhere.

To me as human beings, as citizens, as adults, that's our job. We don't run around and say, "Well I didn't do that personally, therefore I don't have to do anything about that." No, that's not being a citizen of a country. I think that's the real challenge that's in front of us. Are we really going to be what we call Americans?

Interview Summary

Dr. Johnson helped connect many dots on privilege, and the interplay of race and class. We, in the United States, rally around being number one so loudly it seems to distort the ability to see the underbelly of racism for what it is, and how it holds all of us hostage to fear and pain.

His clear example below helps us frame the reality of how we behave about race. It speaks to part of the work that White people can and must do. There are not enough gated communities for all White people to live.

We don't just get to say, "Well I'm just going to own the things that I feel good about in the history of this country that I had nothing to do with. The things that I don't feel proud of that I also had nothing to do with, I'm going to just disown those."

Turning a blind eye to the legacy of racism allows it to continue.

Points for Discussion

1) What is most harmful, racism or classism? Why?

2) What do people tend to be more interested in holding on to, racism or classism? Why?

3) What is the most effective way for White people to discuss racism and classism in the 21st Century?

Reader's Notes

Interview 3

When People of Color

Turn to Self Hate

Put another way, when it comes to race and racism; People of Color–due to the racism that's coming at them every day–begin to believe the lies that are told about them, the messages that are out there about them...and it begins to affect how they are in the world. It begins to affect their life in negative ways.

Hugh Vasquez
Diversity Educator,
Consultant and Author

HUGH VASQUEZ

Hugh Vasquez is a primary cast member in the award-winning film *The Color of Fear* and appeared with the rest of the cast on the *Oprah Winfrey Show*. Hugh joined the National Equity Project as a senior associate with responsibility for developing and expanding the leadership for equity work throughout the country.

He was most recently executive director of the San Francisco Education Fund, a non-profit working to bring educational equity to public schools. Vasquez has worked with hundreds of organizations and thousands of individuals to address issues of race, gender, class, and other social divisions and create environments where youths and adults from all cultures are honored, valued, and respected.

He is a presenter with *Speak Out*, a national organization providing top speakers on social justice topics. Hugh has a Master's Degree in Social Work from the University of Wisconsin-Milwaukee. He resides in the San Francisco Bay area.

THE DIALOGUE

Hugh Vasquez is a leading diversity educator and consultant who helps us define self-hate, or internalized racism, where it comes from, and most importantly some way to disrupt and heal from it. He impresses me as a strong resilient man who goes deep inside of self to examine and root out the impact of racism and gently shows and helps us to do the same.

Where does self-hate about a person's own race or culture come from? Must People of Color assimilate into Whiteness in looks, speech, and mannerisms to be acceptable? How does the idea of "Whiteness is rightness" get attached to self identify?

The signs of self hate have been a root cause in violence, low test scores, job promotion, child rearing, etc. The *Clark Doll Experiment* of 1939 was repeated in 2005, with almost the same results. Well over half of the Children of Color chose White as meaning *nice*, and being Black as *unacceptable*. Are there ways to disrupt this pattern or feeling?

This particular topic is one that is hard for many People of Color to talk about, because at times it's considered airing dirty laundry that may be used against People of Color to validate negative stereotypes. Examining self hate is part of the healing for People of Color to decode what is happening and move forward.

POINT 1
What's Under the Surface of Our Skin?
How Does Self-Hate Begin?

SHARON: Hugh, why do you keep looking so deeply inside the issue of equality?

HUGH: I'm now working with a wonderful group of people out of Oakland, California with the National Equity Project, and it's why I do the work. I am connected with people who are serious about transforming our world and transforming our society. But really, transforming our world so that equity is at the root, instead of equity being at the side of what's going on.

It's been a passion of mine since a very early age. I decided then that I was going to do something about discrimination, do something about racism, and do something about oppression that exists in the world. Ever since then, I've been on a roll working with groups of people who have the same commitment and passion, and dedication to bringing equity to all of us.

It's more than a job. When I really think about it, I talk about it as being a calling. It was a calling that, at one point in my life–having seen what happens when oppression hits people in groups–it hit me directly. I wasn't going to sit on the sidelines and watch it go by.

I've been one of millions who have experienced it. Growing up in a mixed-heritage household (Mexican and White) and the discrimination I saw coming my way directly, and what I saw happening to people around me, was just unacceptable. A lot of people begin to handle the oppression coming their way by trying to sweep it under the rug or pretend that it's not happening. I wasn't able to do that. I had a high school counselor say to me when I wanted to go to prepare myself for a four-year college, that, "Your people are better at automotive school. You think you should go after that?" That was an example of an experience that said, this is not something that's right, not something that's fair, and I'm not going to put up with it.

Self-hate is a part of what many call "internalized oppression." It's what can happen when people are targeted simply due to their race, their gender, sexual orientation, social class background, or age. When people are targeted simply due to their race, they begin to internalize the messages and the mistreatment that is coming their way.

...When you're inundated with the media what messages are you getting about who you are and the people you come from?

Put another way, when it comes to race and racism; People of Color, due to the racism that's coming at them every day, begin to believe the lies that are told about them, the messages that are out there about them, the stereotypes that are out there about them. And it begins to affect how they are in the world, what they do, how they do it, what they go after, what they don't go after. It begins to affect their life in negative ways.

To understand it, I want to give you one metaphor. I want to ask you to imagine that you're looking at a newborn baby in a mirror. Imagine what this baby is seeing in the mirror before society gets our hands on them too much. What they see reflected back at them is beauty, intelligence, worth, unquestioned belonging. They're deserving. They're capable of anything. They see nothing wrong with who they are.

At a certain point, when relatives, neighbors, peers, ministers, police officers, teachers, business owners, politicians, organizations such as scouting, and so on, begin to produce messages about who these children are based on their race and ethnicity, they begin to see a reflection that is dirty. They look in the mirror, and they see something that is dirty. Or they look at themselves as a child now, or as a teenager, or even now as an adult, and they say, "I'm the wrong color. I speak the wrong language. I'm dumb. I'm stupid. I'm ugly. I don't deserve as much as you do." Right?

That's what is internalized. That's what self-hate is about. It's about people believing those messages that are hounded on them daily, and they begin to believe about themselves what others believe about them. The messages that come at them are not coming at them from inside themselves. There is nobody–let me be clear about that there is nobody– who says, "I'm naturally born ugly, or dumb, or undeserving, or the wrong color," or any of that.

That's not how we come into the world. It comes from outside of them, and where it comes from is, I think, a very interesting point of discussion. Some are looking at, "Well, this comes from individuals. My neighbors. It comes from even in my own family. Relatives. Where I'm getting messages that my color is something to be embarrassed about."

It's coming from individuals, but it's also coming from our institutions around us. And when I say "institutions," I'm talking about when you go to school, you are getting messages all the time about your worth. When you watch the news, or when you're inundated with the media what messages are you getting about who you are and the people you come from? It's coming from the outside. It's not coming from the inside. And that's one of the biggest points that we want to make; is that this is not caused by the individual themselves. It's actually promoted and caused and perpetuated by people and institutions who are outside of them.

POINT 2
Why Does Self-Hate Become a Way of Thinking?

SHARON: Typically, at what age range does self-hate take hold?

HUGH: Of course when children get a little bit older, and they're getting into the social scene more, they're going to be interacting in a deeper way, you know, with society around them and with others. Yes, those messages are going to come at them. I think what happens is that we are actually born into a world where this already exists. Meaning, the messages are out there when we're born.

It's not like you're born African American and you have no messages about what it means to be Black until you go to kindergarten. No, you get messages early on. But early on, there is a way that I think young people are able to hold onto their true selves. That part that says, "I'm smart, brilliant, deserving, intelligent," and so on; they're able to hold onto that for a while. And that generally is when they're at a young age. As they get older, grow up, go into the world around them, the other messages start to bombard them.

If they don't have the kind of support around them to kind of fend off those messages, they begin to soak in, if you will. And that's what happens to, I would say, all People of Color. There's a level of soaking in of these negative messages and stereotypes.

I remember very distinctly being in leadership roles as I was growing up, in my community and in my school. Again, I continued to get messages that Mexican people aren't as smart, aren't as deserving. There were a few occasions where somebody said that directly, but mostly it was an indirect message that came at me. But, I began to believe those messages.

The soaking in process is a way that we begin to believe the lies, the misinformation, the stereotypes that are out there about us, and that it affects what we do and how we go about doing it. It affects our belief about our self. It affects our sense of worth or worthiness in the world. Do I belong here, or do I not belong here? It affects whether I strive to get an education or not.

POINT 3
Fitting in...or Not

SHARON: *What is the day-to-day impact of self-hate?*

HUGH: I want to share with you something from Jonathan Kozol's book *Amazing Grace*, because this is a 16 year old who speaks to this point. He writes of what happens when you soak in all of these negative messages around you.

If you weave enough bad things into the fibers of a person's life, sickness and filth, old mattresses and other junk thrown in the streets and other ugly ruined things, and ruined people, a prison here, sewage there, drug dealers here, the homeless people over there.

Then give us the very worst schools anyone could think of, hospitals that keep you waiting for ten hours, police that don't show up when someone's dying, take the train that's underneath the street in the good neighborhoods and put it up above, when it shuts out the sun, you can guess that life will not be very nice, and children will not have much sense of being glad of who they are. Sometimes it feels like we've been buried six feet under their perceptions.

How brilliant that is. A 16 year old saying, "Sometimes I think we've been buried six-feet under *their* perception." This is the impact of internalized oppression. This is the impact of oppression on all of us, but showing up in different ways with different people. And that's what we're trying to fight against and we're trying to heal from. We have all of these young people walking around, feeling as though they'd been buried under someone else's perception.

SHARON: How did you react when you were told, "your people are better in automotive school?"

HUGH: That was a place of resistance, and that's the other good news about this. People do resist the negative messages that are coming their way. I got mad when that happened. I had a response that was basically, "Well, no, I'm not going to do that. I am going to go into a four-year university." I should mention that, at the time, I was actually getting a 4.0 g.p.a. in school. It wasn't that I academically wasn't doing the job. I was.

I recognized that there was something unfair, something that was way off base with what he was telling me, and I mobilized. I mobilized with my parents at the time. I mobilized to fight, to say, "I demand that I'm going to a four-year university," and I would not sit still for that message.

That's just an example of being in resistance to what's coming my way. I ended up going to a four-year university, a little Mexican kid from this very small rural town in California. I was one of only five students from my graduating class who went to a university, then on to get a Master's degree, and to do the work that I've been doing. It's a way of resistance and of fighting.

SHARON: What about People of Color believing the misinformation and the lies? At times, it seems to show up in Asian cultures changing shape of eyes, Middle Easterners changing child's noses, obsession with blonde hair, African American and some Latinos bleaching skin?

HUGH: You know, the pressure is to assimilate. What assimilation means is you move away from being who you are and into being who somebody else is.

In this case, at least in our part of the world, there is a dominant culture, and the dominant culture is the European culture. You gave many examples of different ethnic groups that are trying to *be* White, or *look* European in nature by changing what they look like. I'm sure you've heard this, where students, especially Black and Brown students, and especially in urban area schools, decide that to be successful in school is to be White.

There is a way that some students are deciding to not study, or deciding to drop out, because they think that they're going to have to reject their background, their culture, their blood, in order to be successful educationally. You hear that all the time. You hear students of Color who are doing well in school being blamed for "acting White."

You move away from your community if you become successful, which is another manifestation of internalized self-hatred, right? When people are actually succeeding, and they're being kind of pulled back down, that's an example of people exhibiting self-hatred. I want to highlight a couple things about that.

One, the reason that is happening is because oppression exists around them. It's not the peer or the family member pulling them down simply to have them back home with them. This happened with me, with my cousins, when I was going off to college. There were statements that were made that sounded something like this: "Do you think you're better than us now?"

They were not saying they didn't want me to succeed. In other words, they were feeling the loss, perhaps, of their relative and I was feeling the pressure, the desire, to succeed educationally. I wanted to be sure to return back. My relatives, or your relatives, did not in themselves say, "I want to hold my other relatives back." That's not their intention. That's not their desire. We have to remember that it is outside of the group. The oppression comes outside of the group, and gets manifested in different ways within the group–including holding each other down.

We can't blame ourselves for holding each other down. That doesn't work. What we have to do is look at, where does this come from in the first place? The root cause.

SHARON: *Is there a balance in assimilating into White culture and rejecting it? Does a Person of Color have to be "acceptable" to get various promotions on jobs?*

HUGH: I think it's multi-faceted. It's not an easy or quick answer to that. For example, when you look at the standards of success and what it means to be successful, is there a dominant cultural standard of success? And I'd say the answer is, yes. And what that usually means is there is a White European way of defining success.

Now, what if we had a different definition of success? What if, instead of having success be, "I win, you lose" we have, "we win." It reminds me of when the Native Americans were first kidnapped, and I call it kidnapped, from their families and sent to boarding schools. When they got into school they were helping each other learn. If somebody next to them didn't know the answer they would help the other schoolmate.

They were disciplined against that, right? So, there's a dominant way of being that is a standard of success, and if I am trying to succeed, then I have to know what the dominant ways are in order to succeed. I have to know that. The question is, "Do I have to give up myself in order to get there?" The question is, "If I have to give up myself, do I want to go there?" And then the question is, "Why should that be the way success is defined? You asked about next promotion. I related it to that. Where we are actually being indoctrinated into a win/lose culture, dominant culture, in business and education, in politics. God, just look at what's going on in Congress these days where it is not, "How can we all win together?"

It is about, "I'm taking a stand, and I'm going to win, and you're going to lose." We are all indoctrinated into that way of being. It goes counter to many of our indigenous ways of being. Not just Native American, but many indigenous cultures have a more cooperative value and stance towards what it means to be successful; what it means to actually move forward in the world in a positive way.

> **We can't blame ourselves for holding each other down. That doesn't work. What we have to do is look at...The root cause.**

This win/lose is what we are indoctrinated into being, and this goes, like I said, from the education world, to politics, to the business world, to, you name it. With that indoctrination, then we have to decide, "How do I play that game?"

In order to be successful, I have to learn that game. So I become bicultural, if you will. Bicultural meaning, my culture of origin that is based on cooperation, and a win/lose culture where I have to learn how to survive or thrive or succeed. And my main point is, that win/lose culture is defined for us...not necessarily the way that we are. And I mean "we" as a people.

I think we actually are, as a people, desiring of cooperation, and of everybody winning. I think we really are that way in our nature. But it's become where it gets either beaten out of us, or we get forced into being in ways that are actually against what we are about.

POINT 4
Do Whites Cause Cultural Hatred?

EMAIL: Ron in Dallas, writes: *I think self-hate is a proverbial symptom of the problem with exposure to negative impacts of White privilege on People of Color, and that it's insidious, and dependent on People of Color's strength of character and awareness. They may experience this disparate treatment, but not associate it with racism. Is it racism or something else, basically?*

HUGH: Yes. I think there is confusion about that. This goes to, if People of Color were to really get the healing that you talk about, they would be able to see more clearly what's going on around them.

If White people were able to get a kind of healing that they need, they'd be able to see it, too. What they would see is what Ron is talking about. They would see that racism is there, that People of Color are not making it up. That it's having an impact on them, and that if they're going to attack the problem, they would be attacking racism. Instead, what often happens is that people don't see, as Ron's suggesting.

People do not see what's really going on, and that produces a whole litany of problems and issues.

EMAIL: Mary from Washington, D.C. writes: *Nikki Minaj, who is a singer/artist, comes to mind, a Woman of Color, is voting for presidential candidate Mitt Romney. She has blonde hair, and is so race-neutral. Do People of Color remove themselves because of the ads on TV, and the political environment, and not wanting to believe that they are like the ads, so they sink into some other kind of level?*

Then the media denies there's even such a thing as racism, and it's a post-

racial America? How do People of Color have self-esteem that can function under these circumstances? It's an assault. It's in the face of an assault.

HUGH: It is an assault. I think what she's referring to is that there are some People of Color who decide that they're going to assimilate into the dominant culture in order to make it. There are others who are confused about what to do, and even if doing physical assimilating is the right way to be in the world. In psychology, it's called Cognitive Dissonance, where I see something going on around me, but I can't quite make sense of it. I know enough where it throws me into confusion and upset.

I've worked with many groups in many situations. Some of the hardest ones are when People of Color are in denial that racism even exists. Or denial that it impacts them. People who walk around saying that, "Well, I've never experienced it." Or they say, "Well, what about so-and-so?" Then they point to a leader of Color who has made it. You know? Who has made "it."

They'll point to Colin Powell, for example, or they'll point to Bill Cosby or other political leaders who have actually seemingly succeeded. And they say, "Why can't you be like that?"

The answer, of course, is the dissonance. And this goes back to the messages that if you are to be successful, you have to act this way or that way. And then they point to somebody and say, "If you were to be more like that, you would actually make it." But what they don't talk about is the cost for becoming like that. The mental health. The mental cost. The emotional cost. And ultimately, the cost to lives. Whites also buy into the blonde standard.

POINT 5
Why Black-on-Black Crime?

CALLER: Bob in Detroit, Michigan asks: *The perception among People of Color is not just about People of Color, either. It's the Northern European standard. If someone was Italian-American, meaning European-American and Italian, it's not the same thing. And it's fostered by the media. It comes to the same thing with Tiger Woods. The Swedish blonde White is the example of the epitome, and it's because of this image that so many People of Color have low self-esteem. What do you think leads to this high incidence of Black-on-Black crime?*

HUGH: First, it is absolutely no surprise, nor should any of us be surprised with the level of pervasiveness and the daily barrage of messages that we all get about what is *right* and what is *not*. It should be no surprise that anybody would be aspiring to a European something or other. The problem comes when we start pointing the finger of blame at the individual for trying to be White; for trying to look European, and hold them as the responsible party for that.

What leads to Black-on-Black crime? If you were to ask a serious question about that, and you brought in the concept of self-hate or internalized oppression into your answer, you would come up to a different answer to the cause of it than to point the finger of blame at Black people hurting other Black people.

You would not be able to stay with that answer, that it's "them;" they are just violent, born violent. You couldn't stay with that if you asked the question, "I wonder why it's happening like that?"

We have to be able to ask that "Why?" question, but we have to ask it in a way that's a bit different from how we usually ask it. Oftentimes, we hear, "Well, why is there so much Black-on-Black crime?" Then this is where you hear the dominant culture answering the question in a way that's not helpful.

How does the dominant culture answer that question? They point to the individuals. They highlight Black-on-Black crime in the news. The result is a perpetuation of lies, misinformation, and stereotypes about Black people; blaming the targets. And then you go full circle with people coming back to the answer: "Well, they're just animals."

You have to ask that question in a different way. You have to say, "If I were not to blame the individual, what, then, would be my answer?" What if you took the individual answer out of the equation. What do you come up with? People would have a hard time. They'd look at you like a deer in the headlights, wouldn't they? They would have to look at cause, not just effect.

CALLER: Aziz from Kansas City, Missouri says: *Self-hate comes from being taught by Whites, and we grow up thinking we want to be like them.*

HUGH: If I'm understanding the caller, I would agree if he's talking about that we're being taught by the dominant culture. When he says we have not been taught our history, only their history, I think he's right that we are taught a European history. And it's actually not the truth much of the time.

The dominant culture is saying, "Here's how you must be. Here's how you ought to be. Here's how you ought to look. Here's what you ought to study. Here's what it means to be successful."

What gets connected when looking at other cultures is, "Your culture is wrong, bad, not deserving, not as human, not as smart, not as all that." When you connect those together, that's when you get the self-hate.

POINT 6
Are There Ways to Disrupt This Hatred?

HUGH: I see it in two different main categories. One is that, on an individual level we have a responsibility to disrupt self-hate, and disrupt this internalized oppression. We help people to heal from what's happening to them. We really see it as trauma. If you have somebody who is undergone trauma, there is a whole healing regiment needed. When it's gone on for as long as it's gone on–hundreds of years in this country–we're talking about post-trauma.

You talk about post-traumatic stress disorder. That fits heavily with People of Color who are dealing with racism. There's a way to heal. There's a way to wake people up to what's going on around them, for them to be in community with other people. That helps them to heal. That's on the individual level.

But the interruption also has to happen on the institutional level; in our schools, in our churches, in our politics, in our political arenas, in our social structures. That's why I'm here, at the National Equity Project, to interrupt the systems and the institutions that are, we think, the root causes of this. If we don't do something about both, then we could have some people healed, but the institutions will take our next set of babies and do the same thing to them that they've done to us.

That's why we have to interrupt at the individual level, and we have to disrupt the institutions as well. That's where it takes all of us. It's not just People of Color doing this. It's a collective effort of White people and People of Color coming together and saying, "We're not going to let this happen anymore. We're going to look at how we solve this problem, by disrupting the forces, or the effects, coming at individuals, and we're going to change our institutions so that when these new babies walk out in the world, they're not barraged with messages that say: 'You belong here,' or, 'You belong over there,' or, 'You don't belong here.'"

We all need to take leadership to change this. And this, you know, is in the best interest of all of us. If we have another generation feeling the effects of oppression like all of us have without the healing, and without the changes, then we will begin to lose even more as a human family.

We look at the gains that we have made as a human family. Look at what happened from the Civil Rights days, and the interruptions, not only on the individual level, but on the institutional level, that have made a difference in all of our lives today.

We have better education for all of us because of that. Right? We have better opportunity for all of us. We're not done, by any means, but people can vote tomorrow because of many of those alliances and disruptions that happened on both individual and institutional levels decades ago.

You talk about post-traumatic stress disorder. That fits heavily with People of Color who are dealing with racism. There's a way to heal.

Interview Summary

Hugh was very clear about the poison that leaks into the lives of People of Color who then react and respond to the assault of racism. He helps us to understand that we are inclined to blame the victim when the root of the problem is from outside of the individuals.

He has sobering examples of what the next assault on our babies will be if we don't disrupt and interrupt this old racist thinking. He shows us how good individuals who work hard cannot alone stop racism's violent evil. It will take disrupting the institutions that have become a mighty train engine chugging along a preset track, to do that. It's time to lay new tracks and it requires ALL of us to participate.

Points for Discussion

1) When a woman or man is raped we no longer say, "Well, they were asking for it and deserve it." Why do we blame the victim when race is a factor?

2) What were you told about your "place" in this world? Who told you, or how did you learn it?

3) Can you list the things you like and don't like about your race or culture? What does that tell you about yourself?

Reader's Notes

Interview 4

Psychiatrist Talks
Race and Human Development

First, there are the parents and the family network of friends and kin; and then the teachers. And those are critically important people who need help to think about child development rather than control and punishment, or that kids are bad or dumb.

Dr. James P. Comer
Professor of Child Psychiatry

JAMES P. COMER, M.D.

James P. Comer, M.D. is the Maurice Falk Professor of Child Psychiatry at the Yale University School of Medicine's Child Study Center in New Haven, Connecticut. He is known globally for his creation of the Comer School Development Program–the forerunner of most modern school reform efforts.

Dr. Comer is the author of ten books, including most recently, *What I Learned in School: Reflections on Race, Child Development, and School Reform*, and also served as a consultant to Children's Television Workshop. He has forty-seven honorary degrees and has been honored with many awards including the John & Mary Markle Scholar in Academic Medicine Award, Rockefeller Public Service Award, Harold W. McGraw, Jr. Prize in Education, Heinz Award for the Human Condition, and the John Hope Franklin Award.

THE DIALOGUE

I first came into contact with Dr. James P. Comer's work in the 1980s in Houston, Texas. It was during a time I actively sought information about how to raise my child in a racist environment. I could not accept that anyone would look at, or treat my baby in such a manner.

I found one of Dr. Comer's book, which I have asked him to reprint, titled, *Black Child Care.* In a straight forward question-and-answer format, Dr. Comer helped me sort out some of the most confusing and emotionally-driven feelings about how to successfully parent a Child of Color in America.

Dr. Comer is an iconic doctor in his field of child development and the human condition. During this interview he allows us to have direct access into his current thinking on education and racial healing.

POINT 1
Human Development

SHARON: How did you begin studying human development?

DR. COMER: My plan was to become a general practitioner of medicine in my hometown–a small steel mill, tough little town in East Chicago, Indiana. At the time I went back there to do my internship, my three best friends had started on a downhill course during that period in life. They were as smart as anybody in my class and we went through a really good integrated school.

Yet, the question was, "What happened to them?" Together, me and my brothers and sisters, there were the five of us, obtained thirteen college degrees.

Our family was poor. My mother was a domestic worker. My father was a steel mill laborer. I realized that I needed to better understand what was going on with my friends. That led to me going into public health service and observing, doing volunteer work, and seeing more kids going on a downhill course when society was changing. I realized, they were going to need a better education.

The tendency was to have low expectations, or to control them through punishment when they acted out. That only made matters worse.

That led me from the plan to be a general practitioner towards public health, psychiatric health and psychiatry in work and in schools. I felt we could help schools change in a way they could compensate for what I determined was the underdevelopment, or different development of those young people. And that led to my career.

We're still looking at, particularly now, how you help teachers from the very beginning think child development, and its support for development, and its relationship to academic learning. The way children learn is through their interaction between educators and their environment, and the important adults in their environment.

First, there are the parents and the family network of friend and kin, and then the teachers. And those are critically important people who need help to think about child development rather than control and punishment, or that kids are bad or dumb.

Understand that kids are underdeveloped. Your job is to help them develop. The brain is structured by the interactions that you have with children. That focus on both child development and development or support of teachers is important, and that's what we're trying to do.

SHARON: The brain is actually structured by the interactions children have?

DR. COMER: That's the way it's now understood. Neuroscience has provided evidence that the brain is developed through the interactions between the child and his or her environment. That was not the understanding in the past. It was promoted to accept being born with a certain quality brain, and it didn't change.

Now, we know that the quality of your experience determines your ability to think and perform. Is this to say that everything we do with children as they are developing may determine their outcome and successes and failures in life because of how their brain gets structured? It is both the brain *and* the environment. Destructive things can happen in the environment, but because you are a well-developed person you can still manage.

There's an interesting book about Michael Orr, of the NFL Baltimore Ravens, who is the subject of the book and movie, *Blind Side.* His book didn't get as much attention as the books by others about him. He tells how, as a child, he found the people who could be helpful to him. It was his action *plus* his environment responding to him positively – and his having some talent – that was useful that really made the outcome possible. It was not just the brain alone. It's the environment, chance factors, and many things that determine your outcome. But your brain, and its development is an important part of it.

Is there one or two reasons that contribute to children acting out? The major problem that contributes is underdevelopment. When you have a child who has not had the kinds of experiences that help him or her develop personal control–the kind of self-regulation that is necessary so that he or she can interact with other people well– then, you go to school underdeveloped.

Now, one of the problems is that until very recently we haven't understood underdevelopment. Teachers and administrators were not taught in ways that helped them focus on compensating, or creating cultures in schools that would help children compensate for their underdevelopment. And they saw this behavior as bad or dumb.

The tendency was to have low expectations, or to control them through punishment when they acted out. That only made matters worse. Kids treated in that way would then act up, act out more, and it just went around in a vicious little circle, getting worse and worse.

It is trying to create a culture in which you help children be successful, develop capacities to manage themselves and their lives, and their interactions. Right time, right place behavior, how to think, how to make their environment work for them. All of those things can be taught.

POINT 2
Parenting Practices

If you simply punish and control rather than help them learn, then you're going to get more acting up and acting out. I watched that with my friends. When I thought back about their behavior and performance in school I realized that's what was going on.

The only difference between me and my three friends–who were just as bright–was that I had been taught at home by poor parents. But, they were parents who understood the importance of exposure, the importance of encouraging learning, thinking; all of those things needed to develop. Now, my friends' parents probably cared as much about them as my parents cared about me. They simply didn't know what to do.

One of the things my parents understood was the importance of exposure to things that were exciting, educational, and meaningful. That translated into motivation for good school performance. We were motivated, and we wanted to learn. That is what had to happen. You can't simply pour information into the heads of children and expect them to become educated. They have to take responsibility for learning and they have to take responsibility for their own behavior. It is the interaction *and* the exposure to places that you provide to them.

All kinds of information about how to handle yourself, what you do on this occasion, what you don't do–all of those things are important so that the child gets good feedback from the environment that he or she is in. If the parent doesn't make the effort to make things happen, to expose the child, to provide information about how to handle himself, then the child doesn't receive what he or she needs to be able to manage in given situations.

SHARON: Dr. Comer, maybe a few decades ago or so, this might have been referred to as "home training."

DR. COMER: Right. In a way. And yet you watch well-educated parents or well-functioning parents, even when they're not well-educated, on the airplane on vacation, or in the grocery store. You watch how they help their children perform and behave appropriately. They talk to them. They will explain things to them. They will ask questions, occasionally that help them perform well. Many parents don't know to do that. Their children do not develop as well because they're not developing the language, the thinking, the understanding that's necessary to shape the brain and to develop adequately.

POINT 3
Post-Slavery Parenting

SHARON: Within the, let's just say, African-American community during enslavement, children were taught to be instantly obedient. If a child was not instantly obedient, then really bad things could happen to that family. Parenting practices of some African Americans stem from that. And that the child is told what to do, and expected to behave immediately. There may not have been a lot of room for answering questions or for the child to question. What's your reaction to that?

DR. COMER: I think that was a problem in the past. In some places, and in some situations, even now, that one part of what the African-American parent has to do is to help children learn how to handle themselves. To understand situations and to handle themselves so that they're not self-demeaning but at the same time, they're not provocative in ways that can have difficult consequences. You don't get smart with a policeman on a dark road at ten at night when nobody's around. You have to understand. Maybe you will interact in a respectful way, but you *don't* have to behave in a way that is ingratiating or makes you feel bad about yourself.

You have to interact as appropriate for that situation, and if the policeman is not responsible, then you deal with that the next day through appropriate resources or people in the community, and so on. You have to know time, and appropriate place behavior.

When I say that about African-American children, that's true of all children. Except that it's more important in some situations when you're dealing with people who may have overt or unconscious racist ideas. You have to have the skills to be able to deal with those people appropriately. This does seem like an added burden. Yet, it's simply a reality that you have to deal with, and that we all deal with. Successful people deal realistically with their environment, whatever it is.

EMAIL: Ron in Dallas, Texas writes: *Some Black kids are born into upper middle class, to wealthy environments, and fail at life accomplishments. While other Black children are born into dire environments with seemingly no chance to better themselves, but without much assistance rise to high achievement. Could an explanation of this phenomena be found in genetics?*

DR. COMER: I think it has more to do with your experiences. How you were taught to do just what I mentioned. I have very wealthy African-American friends who will not do their children's laundry, make their beds, and so on. They help them understand that they must be responsible for themselves.

They help them develop with an understanding of what it's going to take to be successful in life. And I suspect that any child whether African American or not, who is *not* helped to develop the capacities to function well, have less chance of functioning in society. The problem is that if you are an African American, then in some ways–not all ways–there are people who will judge you differently.

There are people who are watching to see how you perform. That's not always the case for the average White person, or other people. And that's also changing. You still have to do, really, what all people and children should do, and that is perform at your highest level all the time.

TEXT MESSAGE: John, a student from Washington, D.C. writes: *Studies have found that Black students who start with an inner-city education remain significantly behind White students even if they leave the inner city. What do you think causes this and how can effects like this be remedied?*

DR. COMER: Leaving the inner city in some ways has nothing to do with it. Learning builds on past learning, past habits, attitudes, and ways. If you have a poor foundation and you go to another environment where you still have a poor foundation, what's required to succeed is a higher foundation. You're still not going to be able to perform well. There has to be a compensation somewhere.

POINT 4
Racism is Not About Race: Conscious or Unconscious?

EMAIL: Aziz from Kansas City, Missouri writes: *I'm looking for a straight answer. What is his opinion on how racism started, and what is the solution to fix it? We can't heal if we don't know where it hurts.*

DR. COMER: I agree with that. You know, if you think about the United States, it's a remarkable nation. And yet, we started with two polar opposite beliefs. One was freedom, and one was slavery.

Now, never before in the history of the world have we ever had to justify slavery. We've always had slavery, and there was always abuse of one group or another. In the United States, because we talked about freedom, and human rights, and so on, we also wanted to be a democracy. We had religious underpinnings so we shouldn't have slavery under those circumstances. So, slavery had to be justified, particularly after the slaves became Christians. And the justification was that the slaves, or Blacks, were inferior.

The only way you could maintain that justification was to demonstrate it in a number of ways. That's through overt racist activities and the exploitation of Black labor, of Black people. All that was a demonstration of the inferiority, and the superiority of the White group. That became a part of the American consciousness, and eventually unconsciousness.

Race is very difficult, and very painful, and very useful for some. Therefore, it's difficult to get rid of.

Even as you change the criteria you're always working against an underlying sense or need for it because it's beneficial for people to think they are better than somebody else if they are insecure themselves. Socially, psychologically, economically, there was a benefit in thinking that another group was inferior. Race became the way that we could justify that kind of feeling, and exploitation, and behavior. It remains. Each generation, gets better; but it's still there.

Is this to say that maybe the foundation of the problem of race and racism isn't necessarily about race? That's what I've always said. The human nature is for more privileged people to exploit and abuse others in their own best interest. And throughout human history you can see it. That's what it's really about. Race is very difficult, and very painful, and very useful for some. Therefore, it's difficult to get rid of.

We have a history of abuse that nobody likes. Black people don't like it. White people don't like it. And so, nobody's proud of it. Everybody wants to run away from it, deny it, not talk about it. Yet, it has had some ill effects on both Blacks and Whites. You do have to look at it for what it is, what it did, and yet realize that underneath it, is human nature, and an effort to benefit individually, and as a group, on the basis of race.

EMAIL: Amy in Ann Arbor, Michigan wants to know: *Why isn't racism categorized as a diagnosable mental illness? In my experience, it is easier to deal with serial killers than racists. Why is this?*

DR. COMER: Again, it's the benefit. I'm not sure that it's easier to deal with serial killers. But there are benefits–psychological, social, and economic–in holding racist attitudes. The psychological and social is that you can feel good about yourself. If your personal identity is based on your race, or based too much on your race and not on your accomplishment and the kind of person you happen to be, then you don't want to give that up at all.

You want to believe that it is because of your race–which is a part of your personal identity–you're better than the other person. That's a benefit. That's a psychological and social benefit that you don't want to give up.

SHARON: How can we unlearn racism? Every time we build models or groups like the NAACP and others, and they make strides, we get voter suppression and eliminating economic and social gains.

DR. COMER: It's very difficult to take it on by talking to people and telling people they should be better. What you have to do is to try and create a just society so the insecurity people have decreases. A psychiatrist told me about his own parents, and how they were racist, and that he questioned it. In the environment he was in, that didn't make any sense. As the environment around you changes the early establishment of racist attitudes, and values, are more difficult to maintain.

69

SHARON: Our caller Aziz from Kansas City was saying, "Well, what is the solution?"

DR. COMER: It is generational, but it's also organizational. You know, the organizations, the schools that we're in, the places that we live *all* have to have people who are trying to create good spaces for human beings. Racism has no place in that kind of environment.

POINT 5
Can We Unlearn Racism?

SHARON: Should we concentrate on adults or children in order to fix racism?

DR. COMER: It has to be on adults *and* children, *and* institutions. The institutions we live in, work in, all have to work towards becoming better places for human beings. Be more respectful of each other so that others can be more secure.

When you're more secure, you have less need to scapegoat other people. Racism really is an extreme form of scapegoating. You can speed up the process in part by helping teachers and administrators, and really, all of the people who come in contact with young people. Help young people from the very beginning to think of ways of managing their lives, solving their problems without scapegoating others.

Help them appreciate how their own environment, their own experiences are enriched through interactions and respect *for* and respect *from* other people. That takes skill. You can teach it in schools of education, in wherever we're preparing the adults who are working with the next generation. That's what we should focus on. I have seen it in our own schoolwork, from the very beginning. I remember, when we started our work, there were racists. The schools were chaotic, confused, difficult, and sometimes dangerous places, emotionally and psychologically, if not physically, dangerous. There were a lot of racist incidents, behaviors and squabbles.

As soon as we created a well-organized, well-functioning environment in which everybody could focus on creating a good school culture and good school experiences, most of the racist problems, or racial problems, went away. The covert, on some level, were still there, I'm sure. The most covert went away. When people can focus on the task and accomplish it, and have good experiences, then negative racial expressions decline greatly.

CALLER: Marie from Missouri asks: *Whether they're Children of Color or poor children, how do you get at the lower expectations that educators, or adults anywhere, have of Children of Color or poor children?*

DR. COMER: You have to create schools where that's unacceptable, and where you develop ways for all children to perform at their highest level. You have to organize and manage your school. We've developed a way of having all the adults focus on supporting the development of children.

When you do that, and when you see children developed in front of your eyes who you thought, really weren't able, or they were "bad children" or the like, just watch people turn around from having low expectations and being negative and punitive, to being supportive because they got good outcomes.

You've got to create an environment, a culture in which you can feel good about yourself because you can accomplish your goals, develop competencies that help you do many things. You develop interests that allow you to be successful and where you can have satisfaction and gratification. Then, you have less need of scapegoating someone. We're trying to develop programs where teachers, even before they become teachers, in pre-service, schools of education learn about development. We need to teach teachers how to create environments where they give children the experiences they need. Look at successful school programs for poor children and you will find they often are programs that give the children the kinds of experiences that I received growing up.

My mother had less than two years of schooling. And so, when I became a psychiatrist and began to work in schools, she wondered, "What are you doing?" And she asked me how we were giving the students the same experiences that she and my dad had given us. And she looked at me, and she said, "But that's common sense! And they pay you for that?"

You must create an environment in which they feel wanted, valued, competent, and able. They're exposed to possibilities, they're motivated to learn, and they accomplish. When they accomplish, they feel good about themselves and they have less need to scapegoat other people. This is what all children need. You simply need it more if you're from an environment where you're not getting it at home or in the neighborhood, or in the network with your family.

Interview Summary

Dr. Comer has shown us the inside of our mind and human nature. It's a lot to think about. I wanted Dr. Comer to say it would not take generations to get out of this ditch. He said it would. I wanted him to say racism was a mental illness. He said it was not.

He expertly pointed to what racism feeds on. The oneness of humankind takes on a common reference point centered around human beings of all kindred wanting and doing thing to have the benefits of privilege. Race identity can be a powerful doorway to maintain privilege.

We're used to talking only about White privilege in matters of race. It appears our mental or psychiatric makeup is: Look under the hood of racism or any 'ism' and you'll find a common denominator about the human condition or nature called privilege, and wanting to keep the benefits to feel good about self.

False racist identity seems to be the powerful vehicle to maintain racial privilege. So humans identify more by race than accomplishments and type of person we choose to be. Humans find ways to justify staying on top of another person or group. We see in the U.S. that the notion of freedom and slavery cannot coexist in the same democracy.

It is indeed a long haul. But there is movement forward and takes generations to build a society with firm foundation rooted in justice for all.

Points for Discussion

1) What is the impact of underdevelopment to inner-city children? Can they catch up?

2) Is there such a thing as "Slave Parenting Practices?" If so, was it useful then? Now?

3) What three things are required to reduce or eliminate racism?

Reader's Notes

_____

_____

_____

_____

_____

_____

_____

_____

_____

_____

_____

_____

_____

_____

_____

_____

_____

_____

Interview 5

New Orleans Mayor Talks
Racial Healing

After Hurricane Katrina, we were all under water. I mean, literally seventeen feet of water, and everybody had to get literally, in the same boat. Nobody really cared about what color anybody else was. We were all wet, we were all going. We all knew that we had to save each other, and we did.

Mitch Landrieu
Mayor of New Orleans, Louisiana
Elected 2010

MITCH LANDRIEU

Mitch Landrieu was sworn in as the 61st Mayor of New Orleans on May 3, 2010. He pledged to usher in a new era of peace and prosperity for the people of New Orleans nearly five years after Hurricane Katrina turned their city upside down. As a state legislator, Landrieu represented the Broadmoor neighborhood for sixteen years. As Lieutenant Governor of Louisiana, he served as an executive where he managed a $127 million budget and eight hundred employees.

After Hurricane Katrina, he led the effort to rebuild the tourism industry and the thousands of jobs it created. His team got more than $22 million in grant money from Congress into the hands of hundreds of homeowners, quickly. During his tenure, Landrieu focused on creating jobs. He launched the Cultural Economy Initiative to grow jobs through culture, music, food, film, and art.

The cultural economy accounts for 144,000 jobs in his state where he also worked aggressively to restore public confidence and credibility in the city, government, and police department.

THE DIALOGUE

I first met Mayor Mitch Landrieu when he spoke during the W. K. Kellogg Foundation's, *America Healing* conference in New Orleans in 2012. During his presentation I was impressed by his bold assertions about race and unity, which he addressed with a kind of clarity and ring that few public leaders have the ability to.

I was struck by the gravity of his tone as he delivered his remarks, and he didn't shy away from issues of race and healing. He appeared to have thought deeply about how racism impacted him and his city.

There are very few White men in public life who speak on this subject without compromise or fear. How did he grow into such a leader? What is his story that will help us see a path to the other side of racism?

POINT 1
Urgency- Can We Talk Race?

SHARON: Mayor Landrieu, you have a sense of urgency about the healing of racism. Of all the things that you could focus on, is it more about people, the democracy, or both?

MAYOR: First of all, race is a very hard issue for us to talk about. We haven't really learned how to do it very well. We dance around it sometimes. We act like it doesn't exist. I like to tell people that we're not in a post-racial America, and anybody who thinks we are is not living in the same world that I'm in.

In my experience, the only way to get through racism is to acknowledge that it exists. As I like to say, "You can't go over it, can't go under it, can't go around it, you've got to go through it." We have to have sensitive and sometimes very difficult discussions about it.

When my White friends would tell me about how Black kids were supposed to be, I knew that to be different because my personal experience was different.

It gets to the much deeper issues of democracy, and how people work with each other, and where there's opportunity, and where there's responsibility. Is it fair? Who gets the benefit of the doubt?

How do you really actually get to the essential idea in a democracy that the people govern? Who are the people? Who gets to say? When do they get to say? Who listens? All that kind of stuff gets jumbled up and then manifests itself in policies that some people think are fair or unfair. It's a continual part of our formation that we have as a people in America. We're getting better at it, but we're not there yet.

POINT 2
Seeing the Truth About Race

SHARON: Was there a special moment in your personal life that ignited your desire to break the "don't talk" rule, especially as a European-American White male?

MAYOR: I grew up in a mixed neighborhood–evidently, one of the very few ones in New Orleans–back in the 1960s. I always thought I lived in a mixed neighborhood. My White friends told me I lived in a Black neighborhood.

I said, "Well, I don't understand that." They said, "If you have one or two Black people in your neighborhood, it's a Black neighborhood." I said I didn't see it that way. It looked kind of even to me. That viewpoint was very instructive.

I grew up in what I would consider to be an aggressively integrated neighborhood. As a consequence, my personal experiences growing up were very different from kids who grew up in an all-Black neighborhood and kids who grew up in an all-White neighborhood. I would listen to them talk about people of the opposite race and it wouldn't ring true to me.

When my White friends would tell me about how Black kids were supposed to be, I knew that to be different because my personal experience was different. When a lot of my Black friends talked about White kids, I knew that not to be true because I had a different experience.

My formation was different. I knew the family I grew up in was different. As a consequence of my personal relationships it made it easier to talk about what I saw as the truth. My family comes from the other side of the tracks, and it just got to be something that feels very comfortable for us.

The reason I have an urgency about race issues is because I see how painful it is for people who may have different skin colors, but don't even know that they have common ground. Which is sad, because in my viewpoint we have a lot more in common than we have that separates us. And when you strip everyone down–essentially to what it is that they need in most circumstances–it's pretty much all the same.

That came really to the forefront after Hurricane Katrina. We were all underwater–I mean, literally seventeen feet of water. And everybody had to get, literally in the same boat. Nobody really cared about what color anybody else was. We were all wet. We were all going. We all knew that we had to save each other, and we did.

It was really a beautiful time in a very grave and dark circumstance, where you actually saw the best of human nature coming out. That indicated to me that it was possible. It was unfortunate that we had to wait until we had these experiences to figure out how to get together.

POINT 3
What Comes First,
White Male Courage or Beliefs?

SHARON: *You mentioned this sense of urgency, but you have also stepped into an arena to talk about Race: Where does that courage come from as a White male? Not everybody has that level of courage.*

MAYOR: Listen, it's hard for people to appreciate just a voice on the other end of the line. My father was a poor kid in New Orleans. When he was in law school his best friend was Dr. Norman Francis who later became president of Xavier University, and is one of the most renowned leaders of higher education in the country. Dr. Francis was an African American, however, our families grew up together.

This is not a matter of philosophy or theory. It really isn't a matter of being courageous. It's just testifying to what you know. When there are certain things that you know, you feel more comfortable talking about it. It was a beautiful gift. It also was a curse in the sense that sometimes you hear other people talk, and it's not reflective of your existence. You're compelled to stand up and to say, "That's just not accurate."

The truth is that racism comes from the tree of hatred. It's practiced all over the world, by all kinds of different people. It's not just about White versus Black. It comes from judging people by how they look rather than how they behave. That's just a bad thing. It doesn't get us anywhere, positively. We've got to deal with that and continue to confront each other in a positive way, and move past it.

POINT 4
Get Ahead of Racial Flash Points

SHARON: Is there anything in particular that keeps you up at night about race in New Orleans or America?

MAYOR: There are many flash points. If you're thinking about Whites and Blacks really struggling with each other, you can think about Rodney King. You can think about the episode that we had in Jena, Louisiana in 2006–the scene of a noose hanging that led to racial tension.

You can think about the Trayvon Martin incident in Sanford, Florida in February of 2012, when he, an African-American teenager, was killed by a White Neighborhood Watch volunteer. You can think about a lot of stuff that goes back a long way. And you wonder, why did that flash point happen at that time? What was it that was bubbling up that we didn't pay attention to?

Are people feeling included? Is everybody feeling that when given opportunities, they're given responsibility as well? You constantly worry about that when you're in leadership positions; you're making sure that everybody feels like there's a seat at the table. When you have, I'm not sure it's about just race. You get into issues of how institutions of government affect people that are on different income levels, and what basically happens as a consequence of that. In New Orleans high poverty levels are concentrated in African-American communities.

It constantly makes you aware of having to try to do better, and try to make sure that all of us–on the government side, the private sector side, the faith-based side–are doing everything that we can to close the inequality gap that evidently, in this country continues to get wider. That's a very unfortunate circumstance because it always leads to a dissection and, really, dissension, and people just kind of not having a lot of faith in each other anymore. That leads to dark places, and that's not good.

POINT 5
Government, Race, and Poverty

CALLER: Pam in Toledo, Ohio asks: *What lies in the future of low income people in New Orleans?*

MAYOR: One of the things that we're trying to do is make sure–at least from where I sit, which is in the government sector– that the institutions give equal opportunity to all of us, close the inequality gap and are performing well.

For example, before Hurricane Katrina, we didn't really have a good public hospital system here. It was too centralized. One of the things we've done is create eighty-eight primary health care clinics, all over the city. Now, mamas don't have to wait in the emergency room when their child has an earache. Now, 350,000 people who didn't really have easy access to affordable care now have that in place. That's really good.

We're trying to reorganize our school system, to make sure that every one of our kids–irrespective of ability to pay–has a great opportunity to go to a really good school. I'm trying to make government more accessible and easier to get to, and easier to really kind of move through the difficult bureaucratic tasks. I'm trying to partner really well with the faith-based sector and the non-profit sector, because government can't do it alone anymore because of the very difficult financial times that we're facing all over the world.

Hopefully, by doing that, we're going to create better and bigger opportunities, and more jobs. The unemployment rate in New Orleans is significantly lower than the national average. Our home values are up. A lot of magazines around the country are beginning to recognize that New Orleans has really kind of stood herself back up.

But, again, it's like anything else. It takes generations to fix what has been broken for a long time. Hopefully, we'll make some small progress in the short time that we're here. We're thankful to the rest of the country for helping us, too, because it's really been everybody pulling in the same direction.

SHARON: Do you see a lot of pitfalls and stones that only time can heal, or is there work to do?

MAYOR: I think it's worth stopping for a moment and looking back at where we were in the '60s, and where we are now. I think everybody in

America would agree, or at least I would certainly argue very strenuously, that we have made great progress. We have folks doing amazing things now that they never had the opportunity to do before.

The National Urban League brought their national conference to New Orleans in 2012. Their president, Marc Morial, used to be the mayor of this great city. They had a video, a quick historical reflection of when African Americans came to America. It showed how that transition took place and what happened in the last one hundred years. It ended up with President Barack Obama's picture.

That's worth taking a moment to look at. The individuals in that room were all accomplished and had done spectacular stuff. So, it's worth taking a moment to say, we've made great progress. I think everybody still recognizes that not only do we have a long way to go to get to "a more perfect union," but we have made some missteps along the way. We have to go back in America and look at what made us strong.

The gap in human potential and human capital, the infrastructure gap, the education gap, the health care gap, those things have to be closed. And it's to the benefit of all Americans to make sure that we don't leave anybody behind. That's all of us, together.

We have to build biracial coalitions that create progressive policies that allow us the opportunities that we're entitled to so that our God-given gifts can take us where we need to go. That's going to be a huge challenge in America, going forward.

CALLER: Roland in San Gabriel asks: *What have you observed in your life to be the hardest thing for the majority of European-Americans to understand about the issue of race?*

MAYOR: Let me state the question a little bit differently: *Why is it so* *hard for some people to see and understand the difficulties of other people who may not be like you?* I think we all have a tendency to want to say, "If everybody would just act right, they would be better," as though it's just the responsibility of the other individual.

You've heard some White people say, "Well, we need better values. We need more personal responsibility. We need a better culture of behavior." To a certain extent, I think all of us agree that all over America we have neighborhoods where individuals–Black and White, rich and poor–always and first understand that personal responsibility is really important.

> **I think everybody still recognizes that not only do we have a long way to go to get to "a more perfect union," but we have made some missteps along the way. We have to go back in America and look at what made us strong.**

Working hard, self-discipline, focus, good values, good character, strong families – however people define them – are really good foundations for a civilized society anywhere in the world. It is also true that, that alone is not going to create the kind of union needed to close the gap between people who *have* and people who *have not.*

Sometimes it does take generations. My grandparents had a third-grade education. My father was the first kid who went to college in his generation. All of a sudden, nine of his children went to college. Then, I have five children, and they went. And it took thirty, forty, fifty years.

That would not have been possible without the help of the GI Bill. It would not have been possible without the construction of the Interstate system. It wouldn't have been possible without a school system that helped us get to where we've gotten. I think there's got to be an understanding in this country that personal responsibility coupled with community action, doing things that only we can do together, are important to move forward.

This kind of notion in America that all of a sudden somebody can do it on their own, by themselves, and nobody got where they got without the help of anybody else, is not an honest notion. I think that it's possible, as President Obama said, to not do either/or, but to do both. And I think that recognition is a fundamental premise in order for us to go forward.

POINT 6
A Safe Place to Talk

CALLER: Joseph in Los Angeles asks: *Do you see the apparent code of silence among White people regarding race more a function of class as opposed to skin color?"*

MAYOR: I think it's a function of fear. I think people don't know how to talk about it. This is true – I'm just going to say it – across African-American circles, and it's true in White circles. I think people are kind of circling each other warily and not understanding really how to have a constructive discussion.

I think White people who are not comfortable around African Americans are afraid to speak their opinion for fear of being called a racist, when they may think that some of their opinions are justified. I think that African Americans are afraid to say things in the African-American community where they may be called out.

I just don't think we talk about it as comfortably as we should, because the penalty is too high for everybody. Sometimes we're more comfortable just kind of staying apart. Everybody's had this experience of being in mixed company, and talking about certain things, and then going into, let's just call it isolated company, and having a different conversation.

We've got to get into a room where it's safe to talk about it. Once it gets safe to talk about it, when we all recognize that we have problems, and we all know that we want to get to another place, it's going to be easier for us to get there.

EMAIL: Aziz Bay asks: *Landrieu looks like he has some Black running through his veins. Is he Black?"*

MAYOR: I might be. I'm assuming that I am, but I don't really know. In some instances, it is a biological question, or it could be a cultural question. Or it could be a behavioral question. It's really kind of irrelevant, which of those it is. I think people act the way they were raised. I grew up in New Orleans. It is a very deep, authentic, multicultural place, where we have a lot of different shades of White. We have a lot of different shades of African American.

Historically, we're the only state in the nation who had the flag of Spain flying over us and the flag of France. We are made up of indigenous people and many who came from Haiti, and also Africa. At the time, before the United States became the United States of America, free people of color got around. We all got to know each other really, really well. What we have today is what they call a real melting pot–or we call it a gumbo.

It feels different down here. We respond to things differently than the way the folks in the rest of the country would. And we're not divided as clearly in the same color patterns, or the same behavioral patterns as other folks. That is why this place feels a little bit different. I guess if I could try to explain it, who I am is reflected by where I grew up and who I hung out with, the music that I listened to, the neighborhoods that I played in, and the friends that I had. I am just who I am. Evidently, that is interpreted by different people differently.

CALLER: Rob from Detroit asks: *My question really relates to something* *that I know you have to deal with every day, and that's on the order of racial profiling.*

I've read a lot that some metro New Orleans officials have talked about the increase in the crime rates there as an excuse to practice racial profiling. What's your opinion? In your administration what can you do to correct these views in the city of New Orleans, and in the surrounding parishes?

MAYOR: We feel a familiar relationship with you guys in Detroit. I know that you all have been through it, as have we, and you all are dealing with some very difficult issues. We actually talk to folks in your city about common issues of crime, and blight, and things of that nature.

We have a huge problem in this country right now, with kids killing kids on the streets of America. You see an explosion of violent crime in certain neighborhoods in every city in America. For example, in New Orleans our murder rate is really ten times the national average. Now, we don't have more actual murders than, for example, a city like Chicago and New York, and I'm not even sure about Detroit, but our per capita's a lot higher because our population's smaller.

One of the things that we have to deal with, here and all over the country, is making sure that our police department is well-hired, well-supervised, and well-trained. For those of you who have been paying a little bit of attention, we just signed the most extensive consent decree with the Department of Justice to help rebuild our police department from the ground up.

Now, hurricanes Katrina and Rita really beat this city to death, but it didn't cause all of our problems. We've had some long-standing problems but we've kind of stopped and said, "Look, we're going to take care of fixing the bad things that we have, and we're going to continue to work really hard to develop every one of our policies and procedures." The interaction between a police officer and a citizen is critically important in order to make the city safe. It can't be safe if people don't trust their police officers. A lot of folks who are on our police department are really wonderful people; they sacrificed a lot to save a lot of people during Katrina and Rita. A couple of folks in our police departments have gotten away from doing the right thing, and so we felt like we had to redo it. We're in the process of doing that right now.

Racial profiling is not something that we engage in–to the extent that the policies and procedures would even lead somebody to believe that we could. And at the same time, we want to create a police department that can actually not only serve, but protect. And it's really kind of hard to find that balance, but we're working on it really hard.

POINT 7
What is Enlightened Leadership?

CALLER: Joe from Louisiana responds: *I just wanted to offer a reaction to Mayor Landrieu's discussion. I'm from Louisiana, originally; 70 years old, now. This man represents some of the most enlightened leadership that I have heard in a long time. I think it's that kind of enlightened leadership we need so much more of. It is the kind of leadership that will eventually lead us to a true democracy. The kind of democracy that's been, one man, one vote, all men are created equal.*

Until we can live out that dream, we will never be the kind of democracy we can be, where all people participate at the level of their greatest potential. It's this kind of leadership that I hear in Mayor Landrieu, that tells me there is a possibility that we'll get to the promised land, where we all recognize the oneness of human kind, and we all participate fully in the fruits of our nation. He does not have fear and denial because he's lived among other people, and he recognized, in that time–the oneness of humankind.

That underneath, there's no difference in the rest of us. So, he doesn't have to have fear. He has lost the fear because he lived the oneness of humankind by living with other people and understanding oneness.

I would only hope that, through his enlightenment, he can offer that level of understanding to the rest of elected officials that he comes into contact with. He said, "You've got to go through it." We have to learn to confront it and heal it. That's the reason I think your program is so important, because it talks about, a Safe Place to Talk About Race.

It's that engagement that we must have that helps us under-stand what Mayor Landrieu already understands. It doesn't matter whether you're Black, whether you're White, whether you're Hispanic, whether you're Asian. This takes something away from our humanity, and it's sad that we have been—so to speak—cursed with this disease called Rac-ism. Only through engaging each other can we heal from that disease.

Interview Summary

Enlightening leadership, like the kind Mayor Landrieu displays, is indeed rare. Can it be learned, or must a person be born into a story that provides the opportunities to gain capacity? If a person must be born into a story, or a sequence of experiences, we are indeed in trouble. I believe we can unlearn the misinformation and distortions at both an intellectual and emotional level, but it won't be easy.

The segregation in our society makes it harder to learn the truth and reduce the fear of the unknown. Today, it almost feels like we're being further penalized by the awful era of segregation, and have double the work for all of us to overcome. Mayor Landrieu and the few like him of all races and colors are privileged in a way not valued in the past. They stand as a beacon of how to serve as a pathway to a better future.

Points for Discussion

1) Were you born and raised in a mono-cultural or multi-cultural/racial environment? Has this affected you in positive and/or negative ways?

2) What have you learned about another cultural/racial group that ended up being true or false? And, how did you validate your new-found information?

3) What role does government policy play in the healing of racism?

Reader's Notes

Interview 6

Being Asian:

The Reality, Triumph, and Challenge

I realize that at some point you just have to accept the fact that you chose this as a home. You have to learn, you have to be active, and you have to really help your people–and other people too– to make this a better society.

Evaon Wong-Kim, Ph.D.
Chair and Professor
of the Social Work Department
California State East Bay

EVAON WONG-KIM, PH.D.

Dr. Wong-Kim is chair and professor of the Social Work Department at California State East Bay. She also is a licensed clinical social worker, and the principal investigator of the project *Racial Healing among Former Foster Care Youth*, which focuses on racial equity within the foster care system.

She is an advocate for minority and low-income breast cancer survivors, and is a member of the Intercultural Cancer Council for improving mortality rates of under-served populations. She was a member of Minority Women's Health panel of experts for the Office on Women's Health.

Dr. Wong-Kim conducted research and published papers related to health disparities, cancer survival among Asian immigrants, quality of life and health disparities affecting the Asian-American immigrant and the Pacific Islander population with cancer. She is a well-recognized advocate and researcher for minority and low-income cancer patients.

THE DIALOGUE

I first met Evaon Wong-Kim, Ph.D. in 2010 at a conference. I never forgot her welcoming warmth toward *all* people. I wondered then, how this seemless and fluid woman could maneuver with ease in an open multi-racial setting in ways I'd seldom seen other Asian-American women do?

Maybe this is just the limitations of my experiences peaking its head in my mind, or is there something exceptional that Dr. Wong-Kim knows that breaks through the artificial barriers of race and culture? I doubt this humble yet energetic woman would think she is special in an extraordinary way. However, after you read her interview I believe you'll also share the rare experience of her gifts. Dr. Wong-Kim's show is still one of the most referenced and talked about by our listeners.

Identifying with being Asian and Pacific Islander means many things to many people. Can one name capture the cultural diversity? Are there deep stereotypes and myths that still dominate today? Why?

POINT 1
Are Asians One Homogenous Group?

SHARON: *What is the focus of your work? How did you get so interested in this? What's your story?*

EVAON: I was born and raised in Hong Kong. Back then, Hong Kong was a British colony with not a whole lot of educational opportunities. I was lucky that I had family connections in the United States, so I was able to come to this country with family support, basically, just really live with my relatives.

I was able to save some room and board money, and start at a junior college in Stockton, California. After two years, I transferred to Berkeley as an undergraduate majoring in sociology. During the time as a sociology major I took some Asian-American studies courses, and it was fascinating to an immigrant. We knew so little about Asian-American history in America.

It was mind-boggling that I was so under-educated about my own people who lived in America. All the hardship they'd gone through, the whole Immigration Act that was very restrictive, very racist and abusive to the people, and, how some of these practices continue. We as Asian Americans, have different cultures. However, we're still grouped as one big lump group.

Pacific Islanders have been fighting very hard in recent years to gain their own identity, to say, "Don't always lump us with the Asian group. We really don't have that much in common. We have very different struggles, and we have very different history."

We're supposed to just explain all of our experience with just the term "Asian." The Asian/Pacific Islander, API for short, used to capture just about anyone under the umbrella of at least thirty-some different languages into just the group, Asian. That includes all the Pacific Islanders scattered in Hawaii, in Macau Islands, and South Pacific. It's really a very broad term. I think in those old days, we used Asian/Pacific Islander to make the group a little bit bigger so people would deal with us, and could tell that we had some numbers.

Two, I think it's convenient. A lot of researchers, politicians and policy-makers could just say, "Oh, *this* group of people," although we're a very diverse group similar to the Latino group. Asians from Hong Kong, for example myself, and those from China, versus those who come from Cambodia or Vietnam, are actually very different although we're all called Asian.

Pacific Islanders have been fighting very hard in recent years to gain their own identity, to say, "Don't always lump us with the Asian group. We really don't have much in common. We have very different struggles, and we have a very different history." This term is too broad for a lot of us who do this kind of research. We always really just flinch when people say API. Who are they really referring to? Who are they talking about?

CALLER: Mark in Cincinnati, Ohio asks: *Asians come from many and varied cultures and languages. What bonds them together? Is it government statistic kinds of things, or other things?*

EVAON: I think mostly, it's the service delivery system. I started working as a community health worker and did a lot of work with the community. I saw a lot of agencies that served the Asian/Pacific Islander group, especially at the beginning when a lot more services were needed to assist boat people, or immigrants who are refugees coming to the United States because their country got bombed so badly they had to leave.

During that time, there were a lot of services delivered to them as a group. I think because of that, we came together. Not so much that we share everything in common, especially language. I have no idea what the Korean, Japanese, Cambodian, or Laotian language is all about. It's the service deliverers, community centers and also government agencies, that say, "This is your category. This is what we're going to do for you."

POINT 2
How Do the Diverse Groups Feel About One Another?

SHARON: Another question from Mark from Cincinnati: How does one Asian group feel about the other Asian groups?

EVAON: That's a very good question. I don't know. If you look at racism there are really many different forms. Of course, within groups we have our issues. I wouldn't say we're one big happy family, because that probably will be too naïve to think that everybody just gets along and is happy with each other. There are definitely tensions, and there are definitely issues among groups, and there are, within the groups, some hierarchies.

If you look at historically, maybe starting in the late '70s, early '80s, the Japanese were very strong economically. They were kind of like a dominating society, financially. Then, the Japanese in Asia positioned themselves more or less like a big brother. They were the trend-setter, the ones who had the money and the resources. And I think that back then, there were some ranking in terms of socioeconomic and power. They ranked number-one.

Then things changed. Now, you observe that China has become more of a superpower, though they're still classified as a developing country. So, because of your home country's socioeconomic status, it affects people coming to this country. How it affects them? For one thing, you don't see that many of the Japanese immigrants because their home is doing fine. They're getting the resources, they have food and all of that.

They don't really have to migrate as much as people during the Vietnam War who had to leave because of all the destruction going on in their home country. You see more of those people later, coming to the United States, compared to the old days. You see more Japanese going to Hawaii. There's a lot of issues, diversity, political, socioeconomic, and all of that affects the relationship.

POINT 3
Immigration: Once in the USA, What Are the Challenges?

SHARON: Mark's third question, from Cincinnati: What are the different challenges and struggles that different Asian-American groups face? For instance, what were the main challenges of Vietnamese, and what are the main challenges of Burmese people?

EVAON: The immigration status is a very big factor for us immigrant groups. People who were born and raised in this country have a very different kind of challenges compared to the others who are called the 1.5 generation–they were not born here. This 1.5 generation of kids come when they're maybe six, seven, or eight years old, and face very different challenges.

For example, if you're 1.5, you won't be able to run for President of the United States. Their challenge is that their parents were tied to the old culture, yet they have a feeling of being torn between two cultures.

POINT 4
Do You Feel Like a 100% American?

CALLER: Rose in Michigan asks: *Does she feel that she is different, or see herself as an American totally? Does she feel that she is totally integrated into this culture, now? If so, how long does it take for her to feel that way? This is a very personal question.*

EVAON: It's a really brilliant question, actually, because I ask myself that question from time to time. I think it takes a very long time to be able to integrate into this culture. Acculturation is not a simple process. We don't like the term "assimilation," because that means you give up what you have.

At this point, I would think I am more American than Chinese. When I first came to this country, I think–as a protective factor–I would keep telling myself, "I'm Chinese," so it doesn't bother me, or it's okay for some of the racism that I had to endure.

As a student in Stockton, back then, I remember when I was riding my bicycle home and two guys in a pickup truck threw a beer bottle at me. To me, they basically were saying to me, "Refugee go home." That was the time when there was a lot of Cambodian and Vietnamese refugees moving into that area, basically because the government moved them there. At the time, I would think to myself, "That's okay, I am really Chinese. I've come here for my education. I get educated. I can go home."

That's how I kind of protected myself from feeling that kind of, you know, extreme racism. I could get really hurt, you know? A beer bottle thrown at me could land me in the hospital. I could have even died if I wasn't lucky that day. Later in life, I realized you can only escape so much, to deal with the reality that this is life. I've been here for 30 years.

I have children here. I married someone who's 1.5. He's a legal attorney, very active in the Asian community, and he's Korean. I realize that at some point you just have to accept the fact that you chose this as a home. You have to learn, you have to be active, and you have to really help your people – and other people too – to make this a better society.

POINT 5
Are Asians Quiet About Racism?

CALLER: J.R. from Battle Creek, Michigan asks: *Compared to other minorities, like African-Americans and Latino Hispanics, Asians seem rather quiet when it comes to issues related to racism, discrimination, and marginalization. Is this by design, by the people, or is media ignoring Asian community issues?*

EVAON: Wow! You have brilliant questions, and brilliant listeners. The fact is, there are many different factors as to why we're quiet. I admit that we're quieter than other groups, and we do benefit from other groups' being very aggressive in pursuing opportunity and equality, and other protections in this country. I think, for one thing, a lot of people who come here had very bad experiences with their government.

They were persecuted, and a lot of bad things happened. The Chinese immigrants I work with in my community are very afraid of letting people know what happened, because they don't trust the government. They're afraid that something would get back to their former government. Many of them are quiet because of that fear. You're in a new country, you don't know how they're going to deal with you. You say something wrong, and they might kick you out.

One value that we do share is getting along. That's what I was taught when I was a child. You don't make a whole lot of noise. You need to get

along. That ha~ ~ ˡ . It's not just political. It's space.
.now the minute you step out
ple everywhere you turn. You
e fact that things are going to
ou just deal with them.

other. I would also say, that
portraying a whole lot of
't usually get a whole lot of

...rity.'
...is Up?

SHA... .den pressures within the
Asiar... .d, is this an organized
effort... Asian community?

**EVAO... .r community there are
two gr... h, that's a good thing,
I'm a m... ... I'm accepted by society. I can
move a\ ....a we think that this is a great idea." The flip side of that
is, there's a lot of groups that haven't been able to catch up. They have
not been here very long, and have not had a whole lot of opportunity.
They have a whole lot of problems with substance abuse, with mental
health problems, health issues, lower education, and many of them do
not speak or read English.

Comparing them to the former group, all of the problems of the latter
group can be swept away, because it appears you guys are fine. You are
doing good. Yes. We don't have to worry about you!

And if you look at the statistics, our community really is kind of having something called, "binomial distribution," meaning it's really just two extreme distributions. One group is doing really well economically, but there's another group that's doing very poorly socioeconomically.

Then the problem is, the second half didn't get noted. Meaning, "this is what they call us so they don't have to take care of us." Only the first part took off, you know? They're calling us "model minority," without saying, "Wait, wait, wait, but that's not the intention! The intention was to say, don't call us "model minority" and give us nothing, or pit us against another group."

Some of the literature is showing that some of the African-American groups are very upset with the title, "model minority." They feel, "You guys think you're so much better than us? You are doing so well, and we're not." Then, sometimes, I hear people say things like, "Well, you look at those groups. They don't work hard enough. If they were like the Asian group..." You're pitting one group against the other.

SHARON: *part of J.R.'s question was: Are there hidden pressures within the Asian community, and Pacific Islander community, to live up to these stereotypes?*

EVAON: Yes. I think for everyday life-type people there are these kinds of pressures to the point that people feel like, "Oh, you failed, look at your neighbors, they're doing fine. How come you're not doing well?"

It created a lot more serious problems later. They don't seek help, they don't talk about the problems, and a lot of kids felt like they can't communicate with their family. The expectation's high, the pressure is high, and a lot of Asian kids basically do what they're supposed to do, but not really seeking opportunities that are available in the United States. Meaning, you have to study engineering because your parents told you to do so, even though your passion is in music. I think inadvertently, it really affects a lot of people in daily life, in the sense that not allowing them to make some choices, to bear this burden of having to do certain things.

Then, you have this "tiger mom" thing that came out recently. Somehow it's coined as an Asian thing–these Asian moms who force their kids to do whatever, and then they excel. It's like, really? Does it really come down to that? Something that simple? Maybe it's more complex than that. I mean, having someone who has the resources to say, "Okay, I'm going to force you to play piano for an hour," versus someone who works twelve hours at a restaurant, who has no money to pay for piano and has no money or time to be able to be with the kids because they have to go to work as a dishwasher all day long. I mean, what kind of pressure does it have on those people?

POINT 7
Hawaii: Colonized and Taken By the USA?

SHARON: There is the paradise that's referred to a lot as Hawaii, or the Hawaiian Islands. I'm not sure that our listening audience knows about the history of how Hawaii became part of the United States. Could you share a little bit about what really happened? Was it colonized? Did we take it, or were they willing partners in joining us?

EVAON: I think if you do a survey in Hawaii, you'll get very diverse responses. And of course, a lot of people like what they're enjoying right now. Some of the Hawaiian groups of people are very upset that this is colonization. They didn't have a say when it became a state of the United States. Also, some of the culture has been lost, and language is not preserved.

What's even more important now is that we have the U.S. Federal Government–basically supposed to do something for the other Pacific Islanders – and Hawaii's bearing the major cost of doing some of this work. For example, we're talking about Micronesia, Macau Islands. We have this contract that we're supposed to provide education and health care services to the folks in those islands, because we used them for nuclear testing.

SHARON: The Hawaiian Islands were basically colonized, from what I've read, anyway. The queen was toppled from being the queen of Hawaii, and it became magically part of the United States. And now, Hawaii is kind of a hub for other islands in the Pacific. Do I have that right?

Most of the people in jail are Hawaiian. And, then you look at the Samoans, also mainly in the criminal justice system, foster care, and all of that. What's going on?

EVAON: You have it totally right. Just imagine, you're living in a house, and all of them, they tell you, "Sharon, your house is mine. You've got to move out. It's not your house." You say, "Okay, if you want to share my house, I'll share it with you. I'll move out temporarily, and then I will come back." Then you are told, "No, no, no, you're not coming back. This is my house now."

Some of the people feel that way, that America took their land and their culture. If you also look at Hawaii, the beautiful side is, "Oh, we can always go there, we can blow some money on a nice vacation and all of that."

But, imagine working and living in Hawaii. The housing is terribly expensive, and your salary is really low. People have to work two jobs in order to live there. Even though it's a beautiful place and it's very comfortable, and the weather's great, the reality is, there's a lot of homeless people in Hawaii.

Hawaii is treated as a state, but sometimes it's not. If you purchase stuff in Hawaii, a lot of times, they'd say, "Oh, that rate only applies to the continental U.S. If you're in Hawaii, we have to charge you this, and charge you shipping, blah, blah..." We're treated slightly different, here. We're not totally equal. The distance itself is at fault.

Look at the statistics of Hawaiian people. Most of the people in jail are Hawaiian. And, then you look at the Samoans, also mainly in the criminal justice system, foster care, and all of that. What's going on? What went wrong that even in such a paradise, you still have all these problems? There's still a whole lot of resentment. We don't want to deal with it because we always think of Hawaii as a happy place that everybody gets along; a place that we go and have a good vacation. Underneath all that, you still have a whole lot of social problems not dealt with. The resources are limited.

With such limited resources, you still have to take care of another group of people that the U.S. Government's supposed to take care of. But yet, it ended up being an Hawaiian problem. They're not equipped to take care of more people, when they themselves have a lot of people who are low income, homeless, and only getting by. Now you have the Pacific Islanders you're also responsible for?

I'm not the expert in this area. I'm not a Pacific Islander, and I haven't done a whole lot of research in the area. I have a lot of people I know who live and work in Hawaii, and they're very concerned about how the mainstream U.S. doesn't even know about this whole Pacific Island issue. We are supposed to deliver the services, and the Federal government is not taking full responsibility.

I have a good friend who does a lot of research in this area. The lecture he gives is amazing. We just didn't know the extent of destruction we created in the Pacific Islands. A lot of people come down with cancer.

Think about the island being used for nuclear testing. You cannot grow any more fruit or vegetables, and the fish that you usually eat...it's not edible.

People laugh when they go to Hawaii and see Spam being served on the menu. You go to McDonald's and you can order Spam and eggs in the morning. That must be the only McDonald's that serves it. Spam is so big in Hawaii because when you cannot eat certain food, or when war is going on and there's nothing flying in and your land has been destroyed, you cannot grow any more food.

Even now, a lot of golf courses are being built rather than farmland. What do you do? You eat the things that you can put in the shelf for a very long time, that won't spoil. Also, during World War II, that's what the government gave to people when they didn't know if any supplies would get to Hawaii.

People were given these comfort sacks, and inside the sack there are all these canned foods, so people could sustain their life by canned foods. And this culture continues.

POINT 8
Vincent Chin & the Asian-American Civil Rights Movement

SHARON: *We have a chance to learn more knowledge about the Asian-American Civil Rights Movement and Vincent Chin. Can you tell our listening audience about him?*

EVAON: Vincent Chin is a Chinese-American who actually was beaten to death by White folks who worked in the car industry near Detroit.

I think when he died he was mistaken for Japanese. He was beaten to death because a White father and son lost their jobs. Car-making plants were moving to Japan, and that's why they were angry. After they had a few drinks, they got upset and beat him to death with a baseball bat. I think that was the most openly racist incident that really fired up our community to say, "Hey, we can't be quiet anymore. We've got to do something about this."

That is one major incident that I learned about when I was doing my Asian-American studies. In that class we talked about Vincent Chin, and said, "We need to prevent these kinds of things from happening in our community." We really seriously began looking at being a defined diverse group of people. Even if he's Japanese, does he deserve to die?

I mean, what does he have to do with someone losing their job? That's why the immigrants are often used as scapegoats. When the times are good, things are okay. Some feel, "We don't want these jobs, so you can import these people and they can do these dirty or tough jobs that we don't want."

And then, when the times are bad, some of those same people say, "You took all our jobs away." It's the same thing with a lot of Mexican folks in California who are picking fruit. We need them. That's why our produce is cheap. At the same time, they have a horrible work environment.

You know of those documentaries showing one after another, child labor and all kinds of bad stuff. Yet, we look at them as if, "Oh, when our times are bad, we tighten this up, and you can't come here to get these jobs." Frankly, can we really do this job without them? Fruit picking is not easy. If many of us go under the sun for an hour, we're going to faint. We use these people when we need to.

Our Asian community, same thing. We were being used when we were here building the railroad. There were a lot of Chinese being sent into the tunnels to set off the bombs. And, before they could get out, a lot of people died.

SHARON: *It doesn't just stop with Vincent Chin. Have there been recent incidences of Asian Americans or Pacific Islanders being violently discriminated against?*

EVAON: Oh, yes. There's a really sad case of Private Danny Chen. He was a private in the Army who shot himself in a guard tower while serving in Afghanistan. His death was the result of having endured a whole lot of mistreatment, hazing, and basically ritualistic abuse. His story was all over the news. His parents are really trying to bring all of that out to seek justice. Before he died he talked about how the Army was not friendly to people who are of Asian descent. There was a mistrust going on, and people had been very abusive to him, basically because of the way he looked.

There's also an incident of a Sikh Temple shooting in Milwaukee, Wisconsin. That definitely was a hate crime because its members looked different than the rest of the society. It's just very sad and depressing. That is why it's so important to talk about this– for all of us.

POINT 9
Why Do Asian-Americans Seem Distant From Other Groups?

CALLER: Bob from Detroit asks: *The Asian-American community has contributed much to our society. However, many remain distant. What can be done to bring a closer relationship between Asian Americans and other minorities in the country?*

EVAON: That's a good question. The reality is all politics are local. When we say, "Oh, bringing the groups together," how do you bring them together? How do we reach out to these groups? What have we done to really include those who may not be able to feel very comfortable participating?

I think our group, of course, bears some responsibility. We need to be more active. There are more organizations pushing for more political activism, and retraining the younger generation that, they can't just be living this "model minority" title and not thinking about how to bring people together, and learn from each other.

We are who we are because we're able to benefit from the Civil Rights Movement; we are People of Color, too. If it weren't for Dr. King we wouldn't be able to have all the opportunities we have been enjoying.

SHARON: *I'm not sure that many of our listeners have heard that said quite that way before. It sounds like it's a healing balm of recognition.*

EVAON: Absolutely. Our community needs to take more responsibility for educating the newer comers and people who are not born and raised or educated in this country about the whole Civil Rights Movement. I think there's a lot of misunderstanding, of my people, who may think they have always been able to walk into a restaurant or lodge at any hotel. It wasn't like that just fifty years ago.

POINT 10
Feeling the Pain, and
The New Future Together

CALLER: Leah from Royal Oak says: *I grew up in the Detroit area where Vincent Chin was killed. I was in high school and I remember being impacted so heavily by just the hate that came because of that. I'm so grateful that you're doing this show–so that we don't forget; so that we can move forward. I just had such an emotional response to that, because it just took me back. Thank you for keeping the stories alive.*

EVAON: It is still very much alive, and it's still affecting us. We need to look forward, but also knowing what we endure, we can learn and really understand the psychology, and to think about how we can really prevent more tragedies like these from happening.

I think your caller, and also the people who write to us, and email about these questions, are the people who are passionate about this topic. They need to get to those people who are not listening to the program, or those who turn away when the subject arises. We need to take more of an active approach to preach to those who haven't heard us; those who really are not comfortable, and start a conversation.

SHARON: *That's why we name this show "A Safe Place to Talk About Race."*

EVAON: And I have faith in America. This is a good country, and we have good people who really would go all the way to make sure everybody's doing well. I think things will only get better.

Interview Summary

Dr. Wong-Kim has given us one of the most popular and talked about show aired. A number of listeners have said they learned new information that answered their questions, and more. She has helped us gain rare and invaluable insights into the Asian-American communities in ways the media seems to ignore.

Evaon's voice, expertise, and experiences are a much-welcomed source of knowledge. She opens the dialogue for all to participate and see, once again, that even the so-called "model minority" has not escaped the clutches of racism. Vincent Chin and others have paid the ultimate price of their life, but too few even know who they are.

The testing of nuclear bombs in the homeland of Pacific Islanders has changed their way of life for untold future generations. The colonization of Hawaii and the disruption of Native Hawaiian culture and lands is an injustice still unrecognized. Yet still, Dr. Wong-Kim has great hope for what America can and will be. This can only enlarge the space to continue to share and become greater allies.

Points for Discussion

1) There are many cultural groups in the Asian-American/Pacific Islander communities. What bonds them together?

2) What else do you know about Vincent Chin, the recent Asian-American civil rights movement, and the true history of Hawaii and the United States?

3) How would you build allies within or with the Asian-American/Pacific Islander communities?

Reader's Notes

Interview 7

Think You Know a Lot About Arab Americans? Really?

Arab American is ethnic. It's not religious. We have to separate that from Islam, which is a religion. Not all Arabs are Muslim, and not all Muslims are Arabs. There are Christian Arabs. In fact, we have a large Chaldean community in Metro Detroit. They are from Iraq, but they are an ancient ethnic, as well as religious group.

I think Chaldeans would resent being called Arab Americans to a point, and not all the time, but they are of different ethnicity within the Arab community itself. Islam is a religion.

Charles Khalil Alawan, Hajj
Founder, Islamic Center of America

CHARLES KHALIL ALAWAN, HAJJ

Mr. Charles Alawan, Hajj is one of the founders of Dearborn, Michigan's Islamic Center of America, which is one of the largest Arab-American religious and cultural facilities in North America. A native of Detroit, he has had the privilege of being raised in a multicultural environment. His father, Hajj Ibraham, was from Damascus, Syria, and his mother, Hajjah Katie Ankouny, of Lebanese and French Canadian decent, was from Michigan City, Indiana.

Chuck attended Wayne State University and studied at the American University of Beirut. He has received numerous awards such as the Islamic Merit Award, State of Michigan "Minuteman" Governor's Award for Meritorious Service to the Community, and the Martin Luther King, Jr. *Keep the Dream Alive,* award for interfaith and race relations work. Chuck retired from consulting, as vice president of sales, and as a Muslim Chaplain for the Detroit Area Council.

THE DIALOGUE

Arab Americans know firsthand the opportunities, challenges, and work still needed to help all of the United States better live up to forming "a more perfect union." What do most Americans really know about the Arab culture and contributions?

Is it a myth or fact, that all United States school systems teach at least one Arabic word? Did the Arabs and Islam bring Europe out of the Dark Ages? Do these words mean the same thing: *Arab, Islam, Muslim, and Hajj*? Who are Chaldeans? What is it about Metro Detroit, Michigan that cultivated and built the largest Arab-American religious and cultural facilities in North America?

Charles Alawan, Hajj, a founder of the largest Islamic Mosque and Arab Cultural center in the United States, has lived a rich history in Detroit. He feels fortunate to be a son of Detroit at a time when publicity about his city is sometimes filled with doubt. What does this gifted thinker and unity builder have to say about slavery, September 11, 2001 and so much more?

SHARON: I'm really delighted that we can talk about Arab Americans, the influence of Islam, and to share your wealth of information about this particular subject.

CHUCK: I was born and raised in Detroit. I went to Northwestern High School. I did not graduate from Northwestern. In 1947, my Dad wanted to go home to visit a couple of sisters and he took the entire family to Lebanon, Syria. I attended American University from my senior year of high school through my freshman year of college. I had quite an experience.

SHARON: That sounds like that was another part of the rich experience and heritage that you had the opportunity to participate in, and be that citizen in different parts of the world who brings information back.

POINT 1
Is an Arab a Muslim?

CHUCK: When we talk about this subject of Arab Americans and Islam, a lot of people in this country– still to this day I believe– really don't know the difference even in the meaning of the words Arab, Islam, Muslim, Hajj, and the like.

SHARON: After your name, for example, is Charles Khalil Alawan, Hajj. What does Hajj mean?

CHUCK: Muslims around the world are required once in a lifetime to make a pilgrimage to Mecca to honor the Prophet Abraham. When you make that pilgrimage and you go through the ritual and you meditate and you accept that you will lead the rest of your life conforming to God's wishes and wills, you gain a title. That word is Hajj, which means pilgrim. That's a title we get after we make the pilgrimage. Usually if people within the Muslim community are speaking to someone they will address them Hajj Chuck. In most cases people call me Hajj Chuck. They don't use my Arabic name, Khalil.

When you make that pilgrimage and you go through the ritual and you meditate and you accept that you will lead the rest of your life conforming to God's wishes and wills, you gain a title.

Arabic of course, is an ethnicity, a nationality, whereas Islam is the religious belief. Contrary to the knowledge of most people, there are more Muslims in Indonesia than there are in the entire Arab world. I think the Arab world comprises some three hundred and seventy-five million people. People need to know that places like Indonesia and China have almost three hundred million Muslims. Russia has almost two hundred and twenty-five million. In every country of the world, just like Christianity, you will find Muslims.

Numbers never really meant much to me, but it always proves a point; there are 1.6 billion Muslims and two billion Christians in the world. You're looking at a predominant segment of humankind that follows those two beliefs.

They get the impression that all Muslims are Arabs, and that all Arabs are Muslims, which is not true. There are Christian Arabs and there are Arabs who follow the Judaic faith. I think it's the same thing in most every other country. In the United States we can't all say that we're all Christian. We cannot say that we're all Caucasian.

We have to deal with that. We've been trying to deal with that racial problem for quite a long time. You have to separate race from religion in order to know people, because it's not stereotypical in that you cannot say all Arabs are Muslim, or all Muslims are Arab. It's not true.

Point 2
Media, the words Arab and Oil

SHARON: *Chuck, along those lines, when we hear information coming out of the Middle East it seems to be framed as Arab. Is that our media?*

CHUCK: Yes, that's been going on for a long time. The association of Arab is oil, and the acquisition and the powers that hold oil rights either by force or by legality, have over the years forged the stereotype idea. It serves political purposes. The media has many reasons for not telling the truth, and mythology is not just ancient Greek and Roman.

It also fits the term of how our media sometimes formulates the truth. I was taught there are three kinds of truth: One is white, which is absolute truth; one is gray, which is partial truth; and then black, which is an absolute lie. That's propaganda, and that's the way truth comes out. We deal with that every day and don't even realize it.

Yes, anything that comes out of the Middle East has the flavor of oil rights and it has a political and a domestic and foreign-affairs portion. Let's face it. We have problems in the Middle East. Those problems in the Middle East are not necessarily nation made as much as they are pressure group made. That keeps us sometimes from knowing the truth. We can't help it; sometimes that's the way it works.

Point 3
Unity Building in Metro Detroit

SHARON: *In addition to you feeling like you're a son of Detroit and the fact you've won so many awards related to what I call unity building, can you tell us a little more about why you do what you do?*

CHUCK: I think it was born out of the two years I spent in the Middle East. I was 17 when I got there and I learned more about my own ethnicity, more about my professed religious beliefs, and I got a chance to look at America from the outside. I got a chance to see it as other people see it. The experience brought some things out in me and it made me– I think, a better person for it.

When I got back to America in 1949, I spent some time thinking about a lot of things. I got married, went into the service until 1955, and got out and became an activist. I became an activist on behalf of the Palestinian people because I also was there when the conflict began in 1947. I am not anti-Jewish–God forbid, I could not be. I could not be against God's faith. I am anti-Israeli policies, but not the Israeli people. I always define the difference between politics and humanity. And I still believe there's a great chance for Israelis and Arabs to come to peace terms.

Point 4
Looking at Race in the North

I also began to look at the racial thing. I was born and raised near Grand River and West Grand Boulevard and went to Northwestern High School. I always liked it when my White friends would talk about humanity and the rights of Blacks. I'd say, "you've never lived with them, so how would you know what their problem is? "

You can talk about it. You can read about it, but I lived it. I remember when Detroit was segregated. I could not play in Wingers High School, a school that was half a block from my house, that was for Black students. They couldn't come up to my school, Myers School to play, either.

The only theater they could go to was the Annex. I mean, I'm talking about segregation. Somewhere I have a page of a lease from a house my father bought in 1957, across the street from his grocery store. And right on the lease it said, "Must be sold to a Caucasian." You didn't have to go down south to experience segregation.

My best friend in high school was African American. I've lived it, and I became an advocate for understanding and getting to know one another. And I got involved with a National Conference of Christians and Jews. They didn't even have room in there for Muslims then. It has been a wonderful ride.

Over the years I've stayed pretty loyal to my beliefs. I'm not blind to the frailties of everybody. I don't blame a race for the problems of a few, and I don't blame a religion for the actions of a few. My best friend in high school and I were Muslim buddies, and in ROTC together. We played in the neighborhood together. I had a lot of friends, and like I said, my neighborhood was segregated through the 1930s and up through World War II.

The grade school was segregated. The intermediate high school, ninth grade, and high school were not, because they would gather in the students from the satellite grade schools around the area. I had a pretty refreshing life in terms of knowing other people, getting to know various races and ethnicities, and even religions. Detroit was rich, still is. I consider myself a Detroiter.

Point 5
The Awakening of the United States

I've always tried my best to understand the "other." And the "other" is always someone else besides me. It could mean any particular group or any religion at any given time. I've always tried to understand the other.

Now, I wish Americans would try to understand my people as the "other." We haven't been important at all until we became significant–and of course 9/11. Then, Americans started to go into that stereotypical frame that they have. We seem to like boogie men. Americans just seems to like someone to hate, or someone to blame their problems on, or just someone to focus on. It seems to me that's been an entity throughout my life. That's a little above me in my thinking.

SHARON: One of the things that you said has resonated with me greatly, because I happen to know that you love America. You are an American citizen and you love America.

CHUCK: I'm a patriot. In my lifetime, we had several incidences which brought it home to us. One of them was when the Russians put Sputnik up in space before we had anything up there. That hurt a lot of Americans. We felt it, because we are number one in our own minds. The other thing is when Gary Powers and his "spy plane" was shot down and recovered in Russia; we couldn't get over that. How could that happen? Are we spying on other countries? Yes, we're spying on other countries.

When the Russians were excelling, albeit sometimes with the medical change of gender, we found out that we're not invincible. We found out again in Korea, of course that was because of our own politicians–and we had to bow out of that one.

In Vietnam, we took a hell of a beating because our politicians wouldn't commit. By the same token, I mean, we had a tough time there. We are finding out as the world becomes industrialized and many countries are starting to advance–many of them to our credit– that we helped them do this. We're finding out that other people are in this world and they do have a lot of talent, and that just maybe we're going to have to compete on a different level. And just maybe, they're all God's creatures.

We are the finest country in the world. We have developed a system here that hasn't been equaled in centuries, if ever. Our problem is, do we realize our position? Do we realize that we have to persevere? Do we realize that we have to get better? We just can't sit back and say, we are the best and not work for it. So, yes, I learned a lot. I have had a chance to see things the way they are, and never willing to relinquish the flag. Thank God I was born– and these are not idle words on my part– into the finest country in the world, and given the opportunity to excel.

Point 6
Arab Words We Use and Educate Our Children

SHARON: *Speaking of learning, this might be a myth, or is this fact, that all U.S. schools teach at least one Arabic word? I don't know if our country understands that. Can we talk a little bit about that one Arabic word, or class?*

CHUCK: There's one word I can always bring out and it's, algebra. Algebra's an Arabic word, [al-jabr]. Algebra was formulated and invented and developed by an Arab, a Muslim. It's not the only word. Spanish is, I can tell you, maybe 20% Arabic. Malta has Arabic because the Arabs ruled in Spain and Malta for centuries.

We use the Arabic numeral system. We use Latin figures for our alphabet, but our Arabic system of math, or number, is something that has always been there. I probably could go through, if I had a chance to think about it, words that we say that are Arabic.

Everyday someone jogs my memory and I find another word that comes from the Arabic language. Well, why not? I mean, as I said, from the 17th Century until the 15th Century, the Arabs had developed a government that ranged all the way from Spain, North Africa, all the way across the Middle East, all the way into Iran. And by the way, the Iranians are not Arabs; their ethnicity is a different group. They are more aligned with the Turks. They're not Arabs ethnically. The Arabs went all the way up into the Balkans.

When I say Arabs, at this point you have to think in terms of the Islamic world as well, because the driving force, to drive them politically, was Islam. That's, I think, where we get it wrong in our school books, by making Arab and Muslim synonymous. This isn't true.

Point 7
Arab and Islamic Knowledge Transfer

In fact, during the Arab rule [dynasty/caliphate], the Jews held high positions in the finance system, Christians participated. I think Spain is considered one of the greatest examples of multi-religious cooperation during the Arab rule. There's a vast wealth of history.

It's not too different from the fact that we don't teach much about the history of China, but when you think about the various dynasties in the five thousand years of intellect in China, we teach very little about it. So, yes, we have a lot of English words that are Arab in origin. I also remind people that during the Crusades, the Crusaders were in Jerusalem in the

Middle East, about three hundred years, you just might take something of quality back with you from the Middle East. They did.

They took a lot of things such as a lot of etiquette, a lot of music, math, and even philosophy and medicine. People just are not taught these things, you know. You don't get much credit if you're a Muslim or an Arab in the Western world. I think it comes a great deal from a religious prejudice.

SHARON: There are so many things we don't know growing up in this country, the United States, and that's not really the problem. Maybe the issue is why don't we know?

Were some of the universities that are the source of how we train children today in this country influenced by Arab culture and Islam? Where were those universities?

CHUCK: They were in Spain during the medieval times of Europe, when they were in the Dark Ages and the Church was opposed to knowledge. The language of knowledge was Arabic. The scholars from Europe and parts of the world would attend the university in Spain, in Bagdad, in Egypt, etc. There were schools that people–if they wanted to learn about science, medicine, math, philosophy– would come to those universities and they studied in Arabic. In the meantime, many of them converted some of that knowledge into Latin, and English, and French, and took it home. That's exactly how some of that knowledge came.

I'm just as much an American as anybody else, and I hate sometimes when people will ask me, "where did you come from?" assuming that because I'm a Muslim, more than Arab-American, that I must have come from overseas.

Now let me say this, the Western World took that knowledge in the last five hundred years or so, and we've excelled. We've taken it beyond the state of art at the time. But every history has a phase, and right now it's the knowledge, the science, the math, it's in the Western World. English seems to be the language of commonality. Times change and people move on, and that's how that happened. They studied in Arabic universities.

CALLER: Linda, Southfield, Michigan asks: *I really enjoyed the cancelled TLC show, "All-American Muslim." For me, living in the Detroit area it gave a lot of insight to real Arab-American families and their lives. What did the Arab-American community really think about the show, and what were the issues surrounding how the Arab community felt about how they were being represented?*

CHUCK: That's a big one. In fact, I know the mother and father in that show. I wish I could say I know the children. I think myself, as an American, it was ultra liberal in terms of Islam, and ultra liberal on how their outlook was on certain things. I would have a disagreement. Look, we're Americans. I mean, I'm an American, hot dogs, football, baseball, apple pie, and all the problems that we have.

I'm just as much an American as anybody else, and I hate sometimes when people will ask me, where did you come from, assuming that because I'm a Muslim, more than Arab-American, that I must have come from overseas. In some cases we're sorry to see the program is no longer on the air, but I would think the general consideration on the part of the family was that they were a little more liberal than Islam allows.

CALLER: From Houston, Texas: *Arabs were in the forefront of science and medicine. They had an edge. Why did they lose momentum? What happened?*

CHUCK: Not much different from the Roman Empire, Greeks, etc. I think the Arabian dynasties were about eight hundred years old when it fell apart. It got too large, lost its principles, went from an Islamic moral condition to an immoral condition. I feel like I'm talking about Rome itself. Rome fell, and the Arab empire fell, and I think over for more than four hundred years or more you had colonial powers. Britain, Italy, France, even the United States in a certain way, became colonial or neo-colonialist of the Arab countries, and they've suffered for a long time.

It's much of their own problem, but now they're coming out with the Arab Spring. This is a rebirth, and I think the west is concerned about it. We always look at the bad side of things. I think it's good. I think people should be free, and they need to be free of these tyrant leaders. That's what happened. The Arab world fell apart. It lost its credence and therefore lost its momentum.

POINT 8
Arabs, Islam, and African Americans

SHARON: Aziz in Kansas City, Missouri, and also Linda in South-field, Michigan asks: These questions center around Arab-Americans, Muslim-Americans, and Black Muslims, and Muslims in America. Is there any difference between Arab Muslim Americans, Black Muslims, African Americans, and Arab American communities? How do they get along together?

CHUCK: Wow! Big questions. Let me start out by saying, Arab American is ethnic. It's not religious. We have to separate that from Islam, which is a religion. Not all Arabs are Muslim, and not all Muslims are Arabs. There are Christian Arabs. In fact, we have a large Chaldean community in Metro Detroit. They are from Iraq, but they are an ancient ethnic, as well as religious group. I think Chaldeans would resent being called Arab Americans to a point, and not all the time, but they are of different ethnicity within the Arab community itself. Islam is a religion.

As far as the African-American condition, Black Muslim, Elijah Mohammed founded a religion which was not Islamic in its orthodoxy. It was part Christianity, part Islam, and I don't want to get in trouble, here, but that's all right, I'll venture forth. His son, Wallace, the Muhammad, or in Arabic [Wahesadean 0:40:24] became an orthodox Muslim after his father's death– if he wasn't already.

I believe he was already an orthodox Muslim. Mr. Farrakhan maintained the Black Muslim movement and they are two entirely different movements, but similar in many respects. Islam preaches that Mohammed is the last prophet of mankind. There couldn't have been a prophet of Elijah Muhammad's knowledge. So there are some problems there, so there is a difference within the African-American community. But, the Wallace D. Muhammad leadership–God rest his soul–is orthodox Muslim. He passed away a few years ago.

Are there Arab and African American conditions? Yes, sure. A lot of businessmen in Detroit, and gas stations in particular, are owned by Arab Americans, and not necessarily Muslim Arab Americans. For a few years I was handling the public relations for the Metro Detroit Service Station Association. We tell the gas station guys, "Look, don't talk Arabic or a foreign language in your gas station, that offends people." I wouldn't care if they were talking Chinese, if they're talking in front of me I would like to hear English, to be assured of the fact that you're not saying something about me.

That's a condition of all humans. We used to have problems–shootings, and robberies, and all kinds of problems. And there have been more than there are today which existent between the African-American community and the Arab American dealers.

I think they're learning. I think everybody gets to learn how to get along with each other. These gas station guys put a lot of time in there, and they have a lot of money invested. The Arab Americans said, "Look, we'll open them. We can do this; we can open a business and do business, and hire people." They do, although most of the stations today are self serve, but yes, they were the only businessmen who would go in there and take them over.

SHARON: That is a part of history that needs to be brought out. I'm going to say it this way, Chuck. There was a void in the City of Detroit, that businesses were fleeing left and right, and that void was filled by Arab American businessmen.

CHUCK: The same thing happened with supermarkets and grocery stores. The Chaldean people came in and opened up some of those large supermarkets, and had businesses there. There was always friction between the communities, the African-American community and these business people. There's always a resentment between the "haves" and "have nots," but look, Arab Americans are entrepreneurs. They are entrepreneurs from their toes to the tip of their heads. Sure, some of them would work in the factory, but a heck of a lot more have opened businesses. That's their nature.

It comes from their trading experience throughout history. But there was always a resentment about the fact that, here's this bunch of foreigners making the American dream come true when we can't. There's another issue that I used to meet on regularly, and that is, at one time the banks wouldn't lend a nickel to an African American. We addressed that subject. I was on a committee at Wayne State University going back twenty years where we addressed that subject.

We changed things around by committee and we got not only the banks to reconsider, but we helped found a group that started to loan money, and it was probably through the Episcopal Church there, Bishop Mc-Ghee.

Yes, African Americans were hard pressed. I mean, I don't blame them. They couldn't get a loan if they wanted to. Well, it's coming around. It takes time.

Point 9
How to Reach the Arab or Islamic Community

CALLER: J.R., of Battle Creek, Michigan: *I've been to the Mosque in Dearborn and the thing that struck me, I'm a Christian, the most is how – please don't take this the wrong way – it was very beautiful. But, it was very familiar in a lot of ways, and quite ordinary as it relates to going to other places of worship. That sort of surprised me, based on all of the things that you see on TV and sort of the stereotypes that are out there.*

My question is, in Battle Creek, which is a little town here in Michigan, I do work that's related to race. I want to be a better ally to the Arab community, and I was wondering if you could just speak to a couple of different ways that I can do that. I don't think there's a big Arab community here, but I'm always trying to get people to understand and educate them.

CHUCK: It's ironic. I've spoken two years in a row, this year and last year, in Battle Creek on Islam. In fact, in the last one I participated in a discussion between a Rabbi, a Christian minister, and myself. I'm not sure what your description of the Mosque was. The Mosque is a Jama, the Arabic word is Jama. The word 'mosque' is an Anglicized word; it means a place of congregation. If there's anything holy about a mosque it's that it's dedicated to the remembrance, the prayers, and the gaining of knowledge of the Creator.

Now, I'm not sure what you meant by your description, except that it's both a social gathering place as well as a religious one. If you went into the sanctuary, the sanctuary is where we cleanse ourselves before going in, and we pray, and we meditate. The surrounding element is for our congregational gathering. It has a little different connotation; I think much like a Jewish synagogue, but it differs. The Christian churches today have come a long way since I was a kid. I don't want to spin my subject here, but Christian churches do a lot more socializing, a lot more music, a lot of different things. The churches are not just a building that has to stand there for Sunday; it's a seven-day thing.

As far as knowledge, look, if you want to interact you have to seek out people who are there. There's a group in Battle Creek called, Bridges to Cultural Understanding. If you contact them I'm sure they would love to have you participate, because that's what they do.

The best ways to do it my friend, is to read, and to gain knowledge, and get a better insight of yourself, and then form your goals. Whatever you do, will be for the benefit of the United States of America.

The State Department today would love to have people who speak Arabic fluently, love to have people who studied something about the Middle Eastern history.

The United States of America needs that kind of understanding. We don't have many other ethnic groups, people who are not Arab, who want to and can study the difference and then serve their country. I mean that seriously, serve our country.

The State Department today would love to have people who speak Arabic fluently, love to have people who studied something about the Middle Eastern history. Unfortunately, we wasted our time and now we find ourselves wanting.

Point 10
How to Respect Arab or Islamic Customs in the USA and Abroad

CALLER: Ron of Dallas, Texas asks: *When Americans visit traditional Arabian countries it is required that the local customs be followed, like in some cases, women cannot drive, teach educational courses with male attendees, or be in public without a head covering. Some Arabian immigrants to the United States do not respect our customs, like women are free to marry whoever they choose, and are not subject to mercy killing or disfigurement because they embrace this country's cultural norms and laws. Why is this?*

CHUCK: Let me just start out saying that, first of all we stereotype other countries, and they stereotype us. Most Muslim countries would consider the lifestyle in America to be an immoral one in many respects. We see them traditionally as more conservative. The only country I can think of where women cannot drive or teach courses with male attendees, would be Saudi Arabia. It's the only country in the Muslim world that has that restriction. The Saudi Arabians follow [habi sect]. They are the ultra, ultra radical conservative group. I don't want to get into a lot of trouble, but I think most Muslims realize that they are conservative.

As far as some Arabian immigrants to the United States who do not respect customs, absolutely. Many Americans who go to foreign countries don't respect their traditions. I think our troops are getting quite an education and they're doing a fine job over there. I've heard from several of them that they have a different outlook. But, yes, it's true. Those are customs, and I'm glad you use the word 'some' and customs, and you use Arabian immigrants rather than Muslim, although there are both types that have that problem. Those are cultural problems.

Regarding the subject of mercy killing, most of the mercy killings I have heard about don't come from the Arab world. They come from Pakistan, the Indo-Pakistani community, and are not restricted to Muslim.

The Hindu and the Muslim in those countries have a great deal of cultural restraint when it comes to their women, and they do hold them very tightly. It's absolutely forbidden. The Koran says there's no compulsion in religion. You can't force anybody. You shouldn't force anybody. You should have the freedom of choice. A lot of these things don't emanate from the religious background, they emanate from the cultural.

CALLER: Ann, in Mississippi asks: *What is the approach taken to bring Jewish and Arabs together? How many people go to the Arab-American Museum? And what has been the impact on the Arab people? Is there a lot of support for justice for Arab-Americans?*

CHUCK: First of all, the roads taken to bring Jewish and Arabs together is for Jews and Arabs to get together and talk. And I have, for years. I have many–and I hate to use that–I have many Jewish friends. One of my trusted allies over the years, God rest his soul, was a Jewish Rabbi, and I trusted him explicitly.

It's getting to know one another. It's getting to understand the other person's problems, and trying to come to some solution. The problem in the Middle East could be solved tomorrow if the Israeli people and the Arab people could sit down rather than the politicians; and that's from both sides. I don't care, but you cannot escape the fact that you have hawks, both in the Israeli government and in the Palestinian government.

You have a lot of goodwill there if they would just tap into it and stop killing one another. We are people of The Book–whether Old Testament, New Testament, Koran–we all worship the same God. We can come to some conclusions and ethnicity can be overcome.

Point 11
Why So Many Arabs in Detroit?

SHARON: We ran out of time with Chuck Alawan and I asked him to later respond to why Detroit attracted so many Arabs and Muslims.

CHUCK: The original "migration" to Detroit started with Arab/Muslims and Christians moving there to get jobs the Ford Motor Company was offering around the early 1920s. They were paying a great wage of five dollars a day in the Highland Park Plant and then, later, Dearborn.

There are records of Arab Americans being present in the United States as early as the Civil War. Most of those who came were from Syria, and fleeing the Homeland which was under oppressive Turkish Ottoman Empire rule. Lebanon was originally a province of Syria, and remained so during the French and English Colonial rule. It remained equally oppressive.

After World War I, Lebanon was granted "Independence" in 1937, just before Syria fought the French to gain their freedom from foreign rule. The first large immigration to America came during the '20s and '30s, and many came to the Detroit area. The follow-up immigrations were after World War II – Civil War in Lebanon in the mid '70s, flight from Saddam Hussein in Iraq, etc. During the '30s and '40s I don't think there were more than three hundred Arab/Muslim families in Dearborn, and maybe another one hundred in Highland Park. Look where we are today. Chaldeans follow the same basic patterns.

CHARLES KHALIL ALAWAN, HAJJ

Interview Summary

The rich history and gifts of Arabian contributions to Western civilization seem to get lost. Too often, it is forgotten that no civilization stands alone, but builds on the successes of another. One of the most notable Arab words that every school system uses is, algebra.

Metro Detroit has the largest population of Arab Americans in the United States. The efforts among the Arabs, Chaldeans, and African Americans is the regions are showing progress. There are almost as many Muslims as Christians in the world. Often, people of Arab heritage are assumed to be Muslim; the Christian Chaldeans are an example. The stereotypes about Arab Americans and 9/11 are deeply tangled around religion.

Our opportunity as allies is to continue to build relationships, and seek information beyond the typical headlines.

Points for Discussion

1) How would you define these words: Arab, Chaldean, Islam, Muslim, Black Muslim, Hajj?

2) Metro Detroit has the largest population of Arab Americans in the United States. Why?

3) What are some Arabian customs that are typically thought to be Islamic?

Reader's Notes

Interview 8

Can Sexual Orientation and Racial Healing Coexist?

There's all this kind of really complex stuff that pushes a lot of buttons that are out there. We haven't really begun to talk about that in any kind of discourse in this country, at all. It really divides people unnecessarily, and I think a lot of it is White people's responsibility. It's the way that White gay and lesbian people have fallen into the ditch and have played along with racist notions.

James M. Croteau, Ph.D.
Professor at Western Michigan University

I was expected to marry. I was sent to college and expected to marry a Black man who would be educated so that I could bring the fruit of our labor back to the African-American community. What happened is that I became alienated at school and very down and depressed because I was not fitting in to what I was expected to bring home. I had a girlfriend.

Donna R. Payne
Associate Director of Diversity,
Human Rights Campaign (HRC)

JAMES M. CROTEAU, PH.D & DONNA R. PAYNE

James M. Croteau, Ph.D., a professor at Western Michigan University, is a fellow of both the Society of Counseling Psychology, and Society for the Psychological Study of Lesbian, Gay and Bisexual (LGB) Issues of the American Psychological Association (APA).

His practice and scholarship include LGB issues, race in White Americans, and intersections in race and sexual orientation among White LGB. He received the Outstanding Achievement Award from APA for his contributions. He has written *Deconstructing Heterosexism in the Counseling Professions*, and writes on race and sexual orientation in multicultural counseling.

Donna R. Payne is Associate Director of Diversity for the Human Rights Campaign (HRC). She works with civil rights organizations, religious, and People of Color communities, in addition to leading the HRC's Historically Black Colleges and Universities (HBCU) Program. She received the Rosa Parks Award, is an African-American lesbian activist, and member of the Metropolitan Community Church.

THE DIALOGUE

If you are Lesbian, Gay, Bisexual, or Transsexual (LGBT) what difference does race make? Is sexual orientation in the U.S. "racialized," or linked to racism? How is "Coming Out" as a LGBT person in White America shaped by race? How are the experiences of People of Color with the same sexual orientation influenced by race and culture?

This is arguably the most controversial topics of our times—the trifecta of race, religion, and sexual orientation. How do you navigate the unspoken tension or competition across the backdrop of civil rights?

I first met Dr. James Croteau's during a workshop on race I attended at Western Michigan University in Kalamazoo. I was very excited about his clarity and his kind and inviting approach. He took me to deeper levels of understanding of how White people can push through the barriers of their own experiences and beliefs to help themselves and others.

I later found out that his work included the intersection of race and sexual orientation. The refrain of some was, "Race is too hard. Now the gays are taking the spotlight because people don't want to deal with race." Must this be either, or?

I invited award-winning expert, Donna R. Payne, Director of Diversity with the Human Rights Campaign (HRC) to joins Dr. Croteau to go where others fear to tread in public, or simply don't know how to talk about. Their combined lived experiences and knowledge was profound and energizing.

POINT 1
Growing Up, Coming Out, and Race

SHARON: Why are you interested in doing this particular work on sexual orientation and the intersection of racial healing?

JIM: I think the big reason is consistent with this show. You talked about the ditch of racism that we all get thrown into, and I think that sexual orientation, and how we understand that, and how I understand myself as a gay man, has been thrown into that same ditch.

I grew up in the '60s and '70s in a suburb of Memphis, Tennessee. I'm a White man who grew up with this notion that what was going to happen in my life was going to be determined based on my individual merits. I had a very individualistic perspective on the world, very little sense of where you fit in and how you are treated in the world. I didn't think any of that mattered to me.

...Our image of what it means to be lesbian, gay or bisexual in the world is a White image. It's a White story because everything in our culture is.

Then, as I became aware of my sexuality, that changed. It was a different time in the '60s and '70s, particularly in the South. I literally hated myself for my sexual orientation and kept it a secret. It really threatened to destroy my life.

What I didn't realize at the time, and I've only come to this after coming out, is that one of the real struggles for me was about racism. It was about a racialized kind of perspective on my life. In order to "come out," you really have to realize any negative feelings you're having about yourself due to your sexuality is not yours. It's not your moral character. It's about the way that society has defined same-sex sexuality in negative ways.

That's essentially coming to see the world from a place where you're not treated by your merit; you're treated by the prejudice out there against certain social groups. It's like I had to change my whole world view in order to come to terms with my sexuality. I think we miss that a lot when we start talking about sexual orientation. We miss how racialized it is, and that's one of the effects on my own life.

Another big effect, the consequence of that, is that our image of what it means to be lesbian, gay or bisexual in the world is a White image. It's a White story because everything in our culture is. Everything is defined by that, and so is sexual orientation. That excludes the lives of People of Color who have same-sex sexual orientation. It's all been woven together and I hope we can unpack some of that today.

SHARON: Let me make sure that I understand one part of what you said. That the story of sexual orientation in this country is a White story, as in White European story?

JIM: It is in terms of how it's defined–the image of it. In recent years, there have been images of lesbian, gay, and somewhat bisexual people in the media. Those images are still few in number and they're predominantly White, middle-class, and well-educated. That's not the story of same-sex sexual orientation in America. It's a real struggle to find the image of yourself sometimes, and that's really important psychologically.

Now, I'm beginning to be able to find some images of myself as a White, middle-class, gay man. But those images don't reach the diversity of people who have a same-sex sexual orientation. They can't even see themselves around them so they can come to a positive sense of identity.

SHARON: Is that to say that sexual orientation in the U.S. is "racialized" or linked to racism?

JIM: Isn't everything? Why shouldn't it be? But, we don't see the connection very often, and I think seeing that connection is important psychologically for individuals. It's also really important when we start talking about what to do about all of this, what to do about both racism and heterosexism.

CALLER: Aziz in Kansas City, Missouri: *Race and gayism, doesn't have anything to do with each other. Why are you trying to put them together? The Roman Empire were primarily gay anyway. That's sexual preference. Most of them were White people; it didn't matter what your pigmentation was. This was what the rulers did. When in Rome, do as the Romans do.*

JIM: I'm not going to respond to the comments about Rome as I'm not an historian. I think his main point is that you can't put being gay and race on the same plane to really look at it and try to examine it. At one level I think I want to strongly agree with that, and at another level I have to disagree.

The reason why we struggle with sexual orientation–legally, culturally, and individuals struggle with that–is because we have inaccurate and derogatory information out there about gay, lesbian, bisexual people, and other people with a same-sex sexual orientation. So, in that sense, it's oppression, like racism is oppression.

The push-back that I think is legitimate, is that sexual orientation oppression and race oppression are almost equal. They almost want to say that it's the same thing. They want to say it, and that's problematic. It also involves this kind of thing where, "Well, I'm White so I can say that the racial civil rights struggle is now happening with gay people and happening with gay marriage fights and those kinds of things," and just take that experience and say, "It's mine." You can see that. "I, as a White person, am going to take that experience with racial civil rights and define it the way I want to define it."

There's all this kind of really complex stuff that pushes a lot of buttons that are out there. We haven't really begun to talk about that in any kind of discourse in this country, at all. It really divides people unnecessarily, and I think a lot of it is White people's responsibility. It's the way that White gay and lesbian people have fallen into the ditch and have played along with racist notions.

POINT 2
Racial and LGBT Civil Rights
Any Difference?

SHARON: *Is LGBT civil rights really on the same plane as racial civil rights? How would you answer that?*

JIM: My first answer really is, it's important to know who is answering that question. I think as a White gay man it's really important for me to be able to answer that question and say, no to it. I miss so much if I get focused on gay, lesbian, and bisexual civil rights, and I miss so much of how racism still has such a grip on us in this country right now. I'm apt to ignore that and I'm apt to downplay that.

I think race is central to the psychological and social setup. Racism is central to how we divide people up in this country. We learned it through slavery and all the kinds of racist definitions that have happened since then. That's kind of the primary way that we see oppression in this country and we put one group of people over another. I think that I, as a White gay man, need to be able to centralize race. I need to be able to see and feel my Whiteness, to know what that means for me, to know how it's hurt People of Color, and to know how it hurts me. I've got to see that as central in a way that I'm not apt to do unless I really go out of my way.

I see being gay as central. That was a life and death thing for me. My job is to come to see White as being just as central, and to see how that affects everything else, including my sexual orientation. That question depends on who you are, I think, in terms of how you might answer it.

SHARON: What is this unspoken tension or competition between the backdrops of civil rights? Is this something that we need to really look deeper into for the benefit of all of us to heal with a basic foundation of racism?

JIM: I see way too often those of us who are White and LGBT trying to do education around this. We just kind of get in front of a group of people and we start talking about racism and racial civil rights, and we use it. We use it to promote LGBT civil rights without any regard and any depth of understanding and commitment to doing something about racism. I think that's offensive for some People of Color.

POINT 3
What is the Civil Rights Organization of LGBT?

DONNA: I am an African-American lesbian who actually comes from Jim's hometown of Memphis. I have felt that it was very important to bridge my being an African American into my lesbian identity, or LGBT cultural identity.

I don't believe I have to compartmentalize or box any part of my life in order to be who I am. I am at that intersection of bridging those pieces together. That's why I've been in the movement for over fourteen years.

I work at the Human Rights Campaign (HRC) which is the largest civil rights organization working to achieve equality for the lesbian, gay, bisexual, and transgender Americans. We have a force of 1.5 million members and supporters nationwide. We do grassroots mobilization to bring action in diverse communities and invest strategically to elect fair-minded individuals to office, and educate the public about LGBT issues. That's what the HRC is about.

POINT 4
Growing Up African American and Lesbian

SHARON: What drew you specifically to this work?

DONNA: I have a background in political science and I always wanted to be someone who was very political and part of a movement. I was born into the Civil Rights Movement. I was right in Memphis and it was 1963, and basically everything was breaking loose. During that time, I came from a family that was very staunch in the African-American social network; the backdrop of my life was the African Methodist Episcopal Church.

My father was a minister in the United Methodist Church. I had to adhere to all of the rules–as a good, Black southern girl had to adhere to the rules–of being brought up in a religious family. What I have come to understand is that, even with my background I thought that I would never be able to be a part of the African-American movement, and be accepted. I realized in going through the process of bringing all of my pieces together, that I could be successful *and* be who I am. It was all parts of me.

SHARON: How hard was it for you to "come out? as a person of Color?

DONNA: It was a difficult process. I got a whiff of understanding at a young age, somewhere around age 12, that in the African-American church you were not supposed to speak of LGBT or any type of names as such. You were not to even think "that" existed.

There was a lady in the choir that was a lesbian, and she was bold enough to bring her partner with her on one of the choir trips. My mother said to me, "Okay. Here's what you're going to do. You are not going to say anything about that lady. You won't speak or say anything about her girlfriend. We just don't talk about that, Okay?"

That was my lesson before I got out of the car and witnessed what I later understood was an African-American lesbian couple. When you first understand that you are not accepted in that way, then of course you become alienated from the network, your community. In my African-American community I had a double life going on. I was sent to college and expected to marry a Black man who would be educated also, so that I could bring the fruit of our labor back to the African-American community.

What happened was I became alienated at school and very down and depressed because I was not fitting in to what I was expected to bring home. I had a girlfriend. Then, I lied for about ten years; lying and using a double life so that I would not disappoint the family or the Black church.

POINT 5
Church and Community

When I finally accepted that it was a possibility for me to go to a gay church–I heard through word of mouth that there was a gay church– I moved to Washington, DC and attended that church. But then, I quickly realized that I had to, in order to be a part of the LGBT movement of the church, give up my roots in terms of being African American and networking. I left the Black church.

SHARON: Is that the same kind of thing that happens within other Communities of Color? Is that the same for people who identify as being Native American in this country?

DONNA: The Native-American community carries the doubleness of who they are. There is a name for it in the Native American community– two-spirited. They may not understand you totally, however, they will accept that you are different and they give you a name. In the African-American community there is no name and you don't have anywhere to go.

In the Hispanic culture there is not a name, per se. But, what happens to you is that you become alienated because you can't fit in. You have to follow the strict rules in the community. You are also a part of the Catholic community and your religious part plays a huge factor in what you do. You are living a double life there, too.

POINT 6
Coming Out in the White Community and Race

SHARON: Can you give us your perspective on what it's like "coming out" within the European-American or White community, and how it's shaped by race?

JIM: Donna was just talking about this sense of alienation from her home community; she both wanted to and was expected to give back. With White people, what racism does to us is it tells us, "You're an individual. You're not anything else."

When we get heterosexism or homophobia directed at us, it's not that sense of losing this home base that our whole identity is shaped around. It's a very different experience. That, in part, is the price White people pay for racism. We don't have a sense that we are a part of a people. As a matter of fact, the first time I had a sense that I belonged to a group of people was when I came out, I discovered there was a lesbian and gay community. And for the first time in my life I had a sense of my people. It's a very different experience from that angle and, again, because it's been racialized and because it's culturally different, it's a very different experience.

DONNA: As an African American, you have such a strong commitment to the community because that's all you had in the religious sector. Religion is your political and your social. When you have to let go of that network, that community, because it's all tied together, you become at the mercy of others as they may not understand you and the culture in which you have been raised.

POINT 7
How Does Race Play Out in LGBT Communities?

SHARON: *Is there racism or a need for racial healing within the LGBT community.*

DONNA: There is some need for racial healing as time goes on and I think it is actually happening. But, there's something that I think you need to know. The Human Rights Campaign did an Equality Forward survey of five thousand People of Color across the country in 2009. They asked that specific question, about how LGBT People of Color say they are treated by the White LGBT community.

As a matter of fact, the first time I had a sense that I belonged to a group of people was when I came out and when I discovered there was a lesbian and gay community.

I'm glad to say that, at least overall, about 65% said that you can be treated the same as any other LGBT person. But, what happened when you started to break down how do you actually feel, 47% said they feel excluded a lot of time, or discriminated against within the White LGBT community.

Those were the numbers and factors that play in bringing together all of the community. We have come a long way, but you do have mixed feelings in the LGBT community about whether or not we are all working together at the same time on the same note.

JIM: There are a couple of things there. One is that the numbers are probably a little worse than they look – would be my guess – because the people sampled are probably people who are more involved in the predominantly White LGBT communities, and probably not as many People of Color who are less involved in those communities. You may get a little positive bias to the numbers, but numbers only mean so much.

I think it's clear that there's racism in the White LGBT community. And why shouldn't there be? We are all thrown in the ditch, and just because you're gay it doesn't mean you're not thrown in the ditch, too. I've done a lot of consultation with predominantly White LGBT organizations, and too often, we White people approach it from the perspective of, "I need to bring in some People of Color into this organization."

That's the approach, and people have been trying to do that for a couple of decades now. It hasn't been working very well, because we're bringing them in to organizations that are run and set up for and by White people or White LGBT people. I think some of the work that's beginning to happen that Donna's referring to is much more important. We start saying, "How have we set up this organization? How have we defined what it means to be LGBT, and how wide is that? How much do we need to disassemble that?"

That's the only way we begin to really have an LGBT community that's not defined by White racism. It is beginning. I agree with Donna. I see HRC and some other LGBT organizations that have historically been predominantly White, taking this so much more seriously and really doing positive efforts in the direction and not just kind of token efforts.

DONNA: There is one thing that came to fruition in this study. Diversity may be a reality, but inclusion is the real challenge. That's where it breaks down, actually leveraging differences and valuing differences. That's the challenge we see.

CALLER: Lorraine from Ann Arbor, Michigan: *Is it a double jeopardy to be a Black male and gay? I feel sorry for someone who is. How do they handle it? I would never come out of the closet. Racism is such a huge issue* *for Black males. White males are more accepted because they usually have more money and power of White privilege and position. Does the gay community treat Black males any better?*

DONNA: I would have to actually rely upon the Equality Forward study, and it did point out that African-American males do have a more difficult time in the community. It also stated that sexism is widespread in the LGBT community, too. When I say sexism, I'm directly speaking in terms of lesbians not being valued or leveraged as highly, either.

The Black male double jeopardy actually is spoken of a lot in the African-American community. Then, there's the triple jeopardy for lesbians that is spoken of, and that is Black, woman, and gay. You can toss up and come up with who is worse off than the other, but it is an ongoing conversation that I'm speaking of. It happens a lot.

POINT 8
LGBT and White Privilege

SHARON: Jim, what is your view on White privilege and how does it fit into the LGBT issues related to different cultural groups?

JIM: I think it's probably one of the major factors. For racism to change overall or for racism to change within LGBT communities, White people are going to need to change. One of the real stumbling blocks for White LGBT people is that we're really tempted to see my gay identity as what I am, because it has been something that was a matter of life and death.

The trick then for me, is to be able to see and feel my Whiteness and what happens to me because I'm White in the world. Because, that has to be as central a part of an identity for me as being gay. When it can be, then it starts changing everything. I start finding my own investment in wanting to end racism, and it starts opening things up in ways that don't open up as long as we have only LGBT concerns.

Donna, you might not be critical of this, but I'm kind of critical of this coalition mentality we sometimes have. It has some negative connotations to it like, "Well, gay and lesbian organizations should get together with racial civil rights organizations and help each other out," as if the two issues were separate. Which, by the way, means there aren't any People of Color who are LGBT if we say, "One's working on race and one's working on sexual orientation, and they're separate."

They're not separate. They're integrated so that racism is my issue, and if White people started feeling like, "Racism is my issue and I have a stake in ending White superiority," then things change a lot faster. I think we're just beginning to get there with the LGBT community. I think the LGBT community is better off than the wider community.

I think we've done more work in this area. I work with some local anti-racism organizations, and among the White people working in those organizations, they're disproportionately LGBT–more than ten percent.

I think it's because of what Donna says, that there is a beginning of some consciousness. We still have a very long way to go. I think, especially when you get down into mid-sized cities in the Midwest and the LGBT groups in those cities, they are still predominantly White and they're still not very inclusive.

POINT 9
Ending LGBT Oppression Through Racism?

SHARON: *I'm dying to ask this question. Is this to say, that in order to get rid of the oppression of being an LGBT person you must deal with racism?*

JIM: I would say emphatically, yes.

DONNA: I would add some other complex pieces to it. First of all, one of the things that White LGBT people should know and understand is that as an African American, Hispanic, Latino, or Asian LGBT person, you identify with your race first. Second is ethnicity, third is gender, and last is sexual orientation.

...If White people started feeling like, "Racism is my issue and I have a stake in ending White superiority," then things change a lot faster. I think we're just beginning to get there with the LGBT community.

That is, and for a lot of people a wake-up call. We did the study and we rolled out how people should understand this. It was also understood, from my own upbringing, what I feel first.

The reason why is called, surface visibility. It is how you are seen in the world. That's very important for the White LGBT community to understand.

CALLER: Karen from Washington, D.C.: *Ms. Payne, at what point in time was there recognition that diversity wasn't doing the job and that inclusion was something that needed to be introduced?*

DONNA: For HRC, it began about eight years ago when you had diversity programs that would bring in People of Color, but they never stayed. They just simply never stayed, and, with time we all learned that inclusion has a bigger impact on people staying and being a part of things because they feel culturally comfortable. That's the thing, to make people feel culturally comfortable.

POINT 10
Difference with Diversity and Inclusion

SHARON: About this whole notion of race first as surface visibility. Did you have a comment about that as well Jim?

JIM: Yes, I just really wanted to thank Donna for saying that because I think it's sort of at the heart of why there's tension felt around race and sexual orientation. For White Americans, we'll say, "I'm lesbian, gay, or bisexual first," and we're lucky to even have any awareness of identifying with White at all.

If you use the same notion that Donna mentioned about surface visibility, it doesn't match reality very well, because when I walk into the place where you get your driver's license, people don't treat me as a gay man. People treat me as a White man. Yet, I don't identify with that. That's the heart of the problem of well-intention White people who are trying to work on racism. We don't have a sense that we walk around in the world as White and we need to have that sense. Once we start having that sense then our anti-racism efforts become a lot better.

I think White people need to do the same thing; to say, "I'm White, first," because that's how we're treated in terms of surface visibility. It's very challenging because, coming out as gay saved my life. So, it's very challenging for me to say that race matters and can matter more in my life.

SHARON: Is that to say that surface visibility defines a common element among all the masses of people in this country?

JIM: People of Color tend to be a lot more conscious of that and White people tend to have very little consciousness of it. It's one of the main things that hold racism in place, in my opinion.

POINT 11
Back to Donna's Impact of Surface Visibility

CALLER: J.R. from Battle Creek, Michigan: Why are many African-American churches so intolerant of difference when African American themselves have been subjected to violence and oppression, a lot of times as a result of passages in the Bible used against us?

DONNA: I can tell you that the church overall, has been conservative. Some people have not seen the dynamic of the African-American church, meaning that, yes, they are socially justice progressive, but also conservative.

You've got two of those dynamics playing together because that's how you received the Civil Rights Movement– the Black church came together. You had the dynamics of politics being religion, and religion being politics for the African-American community.

That has changed now. If you watched any of the ballot initiatives that we won recently, you'll note that Maryland had over 35% African-American outreach and they came through and supported marriage equality. That is the first time that you've seen ministers of big denominations stand up in support. The NAACP, and the President supported marriage equality.

POINT 12
Empathy and Oppression

ANONYMOUS CALLER: *What are some promising team-building approaches that might be used to forge productive partnerships between LGBT and People of Color communities? This is the new wider community.*

JIM: We have to be careful when we set up that question. It's a question that says those are two distinct communities. When we say that, we really end up saying somehow that we don't all have a race and a sexual orientation. All of us have an investment, I think, in doing something about discrimination based on both race and sexual orientation. It also tends to render all People of Color, with a same-sex sexual orientation, invisible when we set those up as if they were two completely distinct groups.

POINT 13
Building Alliances

JIM: There's even kind of a deceptive way we of shoot ourselves in the foot sometimes when we start to talk about it. We're talking about it as if we don't all have a stake in both ending racism and heterosexism and sexism for that matter. It's all about changing mentality.

DONNA: You can look at things that are cross-cutting issues, issue-driven pieces that work, support around health care, support around jobs and the economy. Those things ring true to LGBT People of Color and connect the LGBT organizations into what LGBT People of Color are looking at. An example, the Stop and Frisk actions by the police in New York City. The Rev. Al Sharpton held a rally as this is a big deal in People of Color communities. For the first time, LGBT organizations joined him and the NAACP with Ben Jealous, to support the rallies against Stop and Frisk. That's when you see team-building coalition working.

Interview Summary

I hope you are now as enlightened as I feel from this important interview. The taboo has been lifted around that intersection of race, religion, politics, and sexual orientation. We are all beneficiaries of the civil rights movement and all the nameless courageous people who changed our lives forever.

I often wondered what the Rev. Dr. Martin Luther King Jr. would have said about the LGBT movement. Would he have put a stake in the ground around religion or would he have embraced the LGBT movement as another kind of injustice? I found the answer in these statements by Mrs. Coretta Scott King:

I still hear people say that I should not be talking about the rights of lesbian and gay people, and I should stick to the issue of racial justice. But, I hasten to remind them that Martin Luther King Jr. said, "Injustice anywhere is a threat to justice everywhere.

Gays and lesbians stood up for civil rights in Montgomery, Selma, Albany, Georgia, and St. Augustine, Florida, and many other campaigns of the Civil Rights Movement. Many of these courageous men and women were fighting for my freedom at the time when they could find few voices for their own. And, I salute their contributions.

Points for Discussion

1) What feelings come up for you on the subject of race and LGBT? How do you deal with them?

2) We usually see someone's racial identity first. "Surface visibility," is what it's called. Should we *not* see someone in that light?

3) Native Americans embrace the "two-spirited" person. Why don't other ethnic groups?

Reader's Notes

Interview 9

Tim Wise Talks:

A New Demonizing Trend?

I quite seriously mean that I think unless White supremacy – institutional White supremacy on local, national, and even global scale – is not dealt with and dealt with forcefully, and frankly diminished if not eradicated, we're going to have a very difficult time surviving as a productive society in our own country in thirty-five years, with People of Color being half the population.

Tim Wise
Writer, Educator on the subject of Race

TIM WISE

Tim Wise is among the most prominent anti-racist writers and educators in the United States, and "One of the most brilliant, articulate and courageous critics of White privilege in the nation," according to professor Michael Eric Dyson, of Georgetown University. Wise is one of *25 Visionaries Who are Changing Your World,* who lectures nationally, and internationally on comparative, education, religion, and labor market racism.

He is the author of six books, including the highly acclaimed memoir, *White Like Me: Reflections on Race from a Privileged Son.* Wise co-taught a Master's level class on "Racism in the U.S.," was an advisor to the Fisk University Race Relations Institute, and was youth coordinator of the Louisiana Coalition Against Racism and Nazism to defeat Neo-Nazi political candidate David Duke.

The graduate of Tulane University in New Orleans received the 2001 British Diversity Award, was featured on ABC's *20/20,* and is a regular contributor on CNN.

THE DIALOGUE

What happens when government programs for human services are suddenly needed by more White people? Has demonizing those who use services now bleed in a new "colorblind" hue?

Is this new group being demonized for not pulling their own weight and sucking tax payer dollars dry, or are Whites pointing the blame-finger in a new direction that is far, far away from race? Is this part of a make-believe notion about a post-racial America that presses new bottoms rooted in the imagination and identity of many White Americans? What advantage is gained when anyone conjures up and actually believes that we live in a post-racial United States?

Tim Wise is on a mission. The mention of his name among many People of Color raises hope that a White man can voice, with the deep emotion of the oppressed, the truth about what should be as clear as the noonday sun about racism. He offers no apology for what he has experienced and learned through research and analysis. Enlightened European-Americans may at times, pause from the strength of his message, and then take in the importance without argument.

Point 1
Dear White America

SHARON: What is a new demonizing trend?

TIM: I tried to unpack as much of that as I could in my latest book, *Dear White America*. I've talked about these concepts for quite a few years. The point I'm trying to make in that book is, there's an irony to the current economic crisis. Not to dismiss the very real suffering of millions of White men and women and White families, but the irony is that the very kinds of situations that millions of White folks are now finding themselves in is the stuff that People of Color have dealt with generation in and generation out.

They are in housing foreclosures, long-term unemployment, a very inadequate safety net from inadequate unemployment insurance, to inadequate food and nutritional programs, to inadequate housing programs, and public education funding.

> **The economic insecurity that has plagued Black and Brown folks for generations is now coming back on White folks, the irony is that so many of those White folks have for two or three generations now voted for candidates who actually did all they could to eliminate those programs.**

In fact, for the last forty years, the White right in this country has demonized those social safety net programs (really demonized the whole concept of the public sector and the public good) and have tried to link the White voter imagination to those programs with Black and Brown folks as a way to demonize them and scapegoat them for the country's economic problems. Where we now find ourselves–forty years after that process began–is you've got millions of White folks who also need those kinds of social programs and those kinds of safety nets. But, the programs have been cut. They are currently again on the chopping block on the part of an awful lot of politicians, right at a time when millions of White folks suddenly realize, "Oh, wait a minute, we probably need those programs for us as well."

The economic insecurity that has plagued Black and Brown folk for generations is now coming back on White folks, and the irony is that so many of those White folks have for two and three generations now voted for candidates who actually did all they could to eliminate those programs. Here we are, with millions of folks in the same boat and not realizing how the role of racial scapegoating, and really racial resentment, played in cutting the legs off the table.

Point 2
What Keeps You Going?

SHARON: *Maybe we can find out a little bit more about you, and what motivates you and keeps you going on this subject that you've been writing about, and working tirelessly for many years.*

TIM: It's not really all that interesting an answer. The truth is that People of Color have been fighting the issues of racism and institutional White supremacy for hundreds of years. I think as a middle-aged White man in the 21st Century United States– which is to say being White, being male, and being an American in terms of privilege, power, position, opportunity and access– I have somewhat hit the lottery of life.

I don't think I have much right to complain about how difficult it is to fight for social justice when other folks have had a lot more to lose than I have. What keeps me going is the recognition in history of these brave men and women of Color, and White allies whose footsteps I try to walk. And, knowing how much harder it was for them, how much they've gone through, and how much more they've sacrificed than I will have to.

Also, being a parent and looking forward to a future in this country that I think, unless we figure out a way to engage in ally building and solidarity across racial and ethnic lines, we are going to probably not survive as a country and maybe not as a planet. I don't mean to overstate it or engage in excess hyperbole.

I quite seriously mean that I think unless White supremacy – institutional White supremacy on a local, national and even global scale – is not dealt with and dealt with forcefully, and frankly diminished if not eradicated, we're going to have a very difficult time surviving as a productive society in our own country in thirty-five years, with People of Color being half the population.

We're not going to be able to be a productive society if we get to that point and half of the population, which would be People of Color, are still twice as likely to be out of work, three times as likely to be poor, one-twentieth the net worth, double the rate of infant mortality, and nine years less life expectancy.

That's not a recipe for a healthy society for anyone, including my White children and one day, grandchildren. Really it's as much about preserving a society that– as critical as I am of it– I dearly love, and the people in it whom I dearly love. I think this inequality's really not a good bargain for anyone in the long run, even though those in privileged groups in the short run benefit from it.

Point 3
It's Personal

SHARON: Not only is it about that kind of future, but future for your children and grandchildren as well. When did it get really personal?

TIM: For me – and I think like a lot of White folks in particular – our introduction to these concepts of oppression and injustice are sometimes rather academic to the way People of Color experience them. That's not to say that there aren't an awful lot of poor and struggling White folks who actually do have an experience of economic oppression. But I grew up like most White Americans, which is to say that even though my family didn't have a whole lot, we certainly weren't oppressed or marginalized.

My introduction to it would have been somewhat academic. I went to college in New Orleans, Louisiana, and after graduating I worked as a community organizer in mostly low-income Communities of Color there. I really got to meet the people who were every single day against great odds, trying to raise their families and put food on the table. They were trying to go to work, or if they didn't have a job, find a job, find some way to keep it together in spite of economic and racial odds being completely stacked against them.

It was unbelievably inspiring. It was very personal, because the people I met were some of the most wisdom-filled people I'd ever met, even though their formal education wasn't all that impressive. Even though most people in this country wouldn't give them a whole lot of credit for being particularly 'smart.'

Whatever book smarts they may or may not have had, they were incredibly wise people. What was jarring to me about that was I, like most folks, no matter how liberal or progressive our political views, had still been led to believe that the people in those communities weren't all the evil as the media cast them. I still believed that they were somewhat helpless, or needed to be helped.

It was getting to know folks and realizing, "My God, these are people that actually understand the political system a lot better than I do, and I've got a college degree. These are people that have a lot more understanding of the economic system than I do, and I studied all those things." It really flipped my world upside-down and congealed at a very particular time when these things stopped being academic for me and started being quite a bit more personal.

SHARON: I'm hoping very much that there are more people in the United States of any background, culture or so-called race, who can go from that academic head right straight to the heart of the matter.

TIM: That was part of it for me. It was all over the course of four or five years. Around that same time, I graduated from Tulane University in 1990. And in Louisiana at that time, David Duke, a White supremacist and former Ku Klux Klan leader, was running for the United States Senate.

He'd already won a seat in the State Legislature when two friends and colleagues from college were part of an organization to lead the charge against Duke. I was hired right out of college to be involved in that work. I did that work for two years, both during the Senate race and then after Duke was defeated in that race he ran for governor. So, I was involved in the anti-Duke coalition for the governor's race as well. That was another thing that really, for me I think, made it personal.

Because at the end of the day, with the help of 88% turnout in the Black community, that really was what made the difference in defeating Duke. Nonetheless, even though we were able to defeat him he did manage to get a seat on the Senate in 1990 with 60% White vote. Six out of ten White voters.

During the governor's race in 1991, he got 55% of the White vote. What this meant to me at the age of 23, is that roughly six out of ten people who check off the census boxes the same way I do, who are White like I am, voted for a guy who they knew was a Nazi. It's not as if they didn't know. There's no way you couldn't have known. Everybody in the United States knew. This was a national and international story. Everyone in Louisiana knew what this guy was and what he believed in, and yet six out of ten people at the end of the day basically said, "Oh well. Yeah, he's a Nazi, but gee, I prefer him to the other guy."

I just remember thinking, "What does it say?" I knew that six out of ten White people in that state were not themselves Nazis. I knew that they weren't. I knew that they weren't six out of ten bigoted, hateful Klansmen or something, but they were willing to vote for a guy who was all of that. To me, I had to really reflect on what separated me from them. I wasn't any better than them in a sense of being more moral or necessarily more wonderful human being. The only difference that I could really come up with was I had a certain set of experiences growing up. I'd been raised one particular way and had certain views, and they'd been raised a very different way and they'd had different experiences.

They weren't to blame for their upbringing and their experiences. I was just fortunate to have parents who led me away from Nazism and away from White supremacist thinking. That was the moment I realized there was this sickness permeating my people. It wasn't because they were bad; most of them were good. But, good people were capable of doing some really fundamentally horrific things like, voting for David Duke.

Point 4
The White Imagination

SHARON: *One of the points that comes up has to do with White identity and imagination. Can you talk a little bit about that for a moment in the context of this new demonizing trend or White or European Americans who are in a new hard economic circumstance?*

TIM: I'll try to put it in some historical perspective. The "funny" thing–and again, I'm using "funny" in quotes because it's not all that humorous–about this resurgence of anti-government, anti-public service, anti-social safety net program mentality is that it's really quite new for White Americans. We forget that sixty, or seventy years ago, during the Great Depression and shortly thereafter, there was really widespread support among virtually all folks in this country–except for the very wealthy– for large government intervention in the housing markets with the FHA, GI Bills, enhanced public education and loans for college, and the VA loan programs. These really created the middle class.

There was just widespread agreement among the so-called working class or what we might now call the middle or lower middle class, that sometimes the market just didn't work, and the state needed to intervene. Now, rich people didn't feel that way because they wanted people to have to work for them at whatever lousy wage they were willing to pay. The ultra-wealthy then felt pretty much the way I guess many of them do now. Everyone else realized there was a role to play for government intervention.

The Republican platform of 1956, actually was militantly pro-union. It talked about the importance of the state. We see how much it's changed. What's changed, and what I think Americans need to get their head around, particularly in a political season like the one we're in now, is why did we all of a sudden turn against those things? There are sociologists who have looked at the way that discussions about anti-poverty efforts, about government intervention in the housing markets and the job markets, all of a sudden switched from generally being positive, toward being a negative view of those things.

It begins really, in the late 1960s and early 1970s. What happens between let's say the '30s and '40s on one hand and the '60s and '70s on the other? Well, what happens is that all of a sudden People of Color, who had been blocked from all of those government programs in the earliest days, blocked from the FHA and the VA loans, had been highly limited in their ability to use the GI Bill, blocked from the AFDC, or what then was called the ADC program, main cash flow program.

We turned against the notion of government support for those in need. And for the last forty years there's been that constant repetition of that symbolism that somehow when we talk about helping the have not's or the have lessor's, the assumption in the White imagination – and frankly even in the imaginations of some folks of Color – is that we're talking about *taking* from White people and *giving* to People of Color.

When in fact of course, millions of White folks have always depended upon those programs in times of need, and right now, when the job market is in the situation it is, when the housing market is where it's been for several years, White folks too needed those very programs. The scapegoating of People of Color and those programs and the associations of those efforts with People of Color has helped to reduce support for them.

In fact, there's been some fascinating international studies, which have found that the primary thing, the number-one factor differentiating the United States from the other western, industrialized nations that we like to compare ourselves to, is guaranteed national health care. The biggest single factor in those studies is the belief of White folks that, if we have bigger programs like that, Black and Brown folks will abuse them.

In other words, the irony is that White folks are so obsessed with the notion that People of Color are going to get something over on us, going to get something for nothing, that we're actually willing to cut programs or never even implement programs that we could benefit from, just to keep other people from "taking advantage" of them. It's really somewhat psychotic, and it's leading to a safety net that is just utterly Swiss-cheese like in its orientation.

Point 5
The New Blame Finger? The President?

SHARON: Where is the blame finger now being pointed? Is it going someplace else as well or is it still stuck on People of Color?

TIM: It's still very much stuck on People of Color. Of course with a Black president, it's very easy symbolically for commentators who wish to scapegoat the poor and the working class to especially push those buttons of racial resentment. Without even really saying it, they can just suggest that this President, especially because he's a person of Color, is going to bend over backwards for "those people."

In fact, there's a video of Mitt Romney at a fund raiser talking to donors behind closed doors. He said that 47% of Americans will vote for President Barack Obama no matter what because they're dependent on government, they believe they're victims, and that government has the responsibility to care for them. And, they believe they're entitled to health care, to food, and to housing.

Now, he doesn't say that these people are all Black. And, of course they wouldn't all be Black, they wouldn't all be People of Color. There would be an awful lot of White folks, too. We talk about 47% of the population. That whole notion that 47% of the population are dependent on government, aside from being absurd, it isn't true. That's ridiculous. That includes people that are dependent in the sense only that they might be elderly and get Medicare benefits.

They might be elderly and get Medicaid Part D prescription drug benefits. They might get the Earned Income Tax credit–God forbid, which is a program that even Ronald Reagan used to support. They might get the deductible refundable childcare tax credit. They might use the Head

Start program. Or, they might get Pell Grants. Eight million college students get Pell Grants. That's not being dependent on government, it's taking advantage of programs you've paid for vis-a-vis tax dollars.

It's an ignorant statement number one. But, it's also racially coded in the sense that we know that when we talk about people who are "dependent on government," study after study has told us for years what people imagine when they hear that phrase. In other words, when you say "welfare dependency," you say dependent on the state, and what people see–whether or not you intended–is a Person of Color.

The biggest single factor in those studies is the belief of White folks that, if we have bigger programs like that, Black and Brown folks will abuse them. In other words, the irony is that White folks are so obsessed with the notion that People of Color are going to get something over on us.

There are at least six or seven studies that have found that to be true. If that's what people are hearing, it's fundamentally irresponsible for folks to use that kind of phraseology, because they have to know that that's what people are hearing. It becomes this dog whistle way in which people can speak about race, and speak about racial others, without ever having to actually call it out.

Occasionally, they will slip as did *Fox News* host, Greg Gutfeld, who is on a couple of Fox programs. A couple of weeks ago during the Republican convention, he actually made this argument. He's a White guy who's talking about Mia Love, the Black Mormon candidate for Congress in one of the districts in Utah. He was talking about her and contrasting her with Black folks generally, and he was saying how great she was because she can be the one to remind people that the Democratic party has basically made an entire race dependent on government. He's obviously talking about Black people. The only context of this conversation, was about African Americans.

184

He makes that comment, as if somehow Black people are dependent on government. Not only is that incredibly racist in the sense that it denigrates an entire group of people for supposedly being dependent and lazy and slothful, but it's wrong. The fact is, contrary to popular belief. If you were to take all the Black adults in this country who actually receive any cash welfare benefits at all, you would be looking at less than 400,000 who receive cash welfare in the course of a given year.

That's less than 400,000 people in a nation of 29 million African-American adults. We're talking about a small portion of the population. But, when folks use that kind of phraseology, they know it gins up racial anxiety, racial resentment, makes White people angry; makes them think they're getting taking advantage of. It has everything to do with pushing buttons of anger, resentment, and racial hostility.

Point 6
Emotions: Facts Versus Fiction

SHARON: This is some old encoding that seems to not go away. We've heard these thing for years, and part of what we like to do with the healing of racism is call it what it is. And, as you say too, unpack it in a way that people will understand. I'm struck with this part of the imagination. Obviously, you do your homework. You looked up the data, but the messages in the larger society don't seem to change.

TIM: That's just it. There's a lot of research on this too, which unfortunately is very demoralizing for those of us who think that facts ought to matter. What the research actually finds is sad when it comes to issues that are highly emotionally charged, and God knows racial issues are, gender issues are, class issues are, religious issues are, that those are issues where the facts mean absolutely nothing to swaying people.

People are dug into what they believe to be true. In fact, some research has found that when you present the facts, the hard, true evidence to someone who's really committed to believing the opposite of what the truth is, they actually dig in harder.

Not only do they not get persuaded, they actually will become more resolute, ever more convinced that they are right and that you are wrong. This poses a real challenge, and I don't think any of us have quite figured out how to deal with that.

How do you deal with people who are impervious to facts? How do you deal with people who actually want to believe something that, whether it's science or whether it's social science, says it's not true. What do you do? I'd love to tell you I have the answer to that. I don't really know, but I think that's the challenge. Because people can lie about poor folks, they can lie about People of Color, they can lie about immigrants, they can lie about all kinds of things.

There are large numbers of the American population who apparently are wired to believe the lies. We're going to have to figure out some cognitive strategy, I don't know, some rhetorical strategy, some type of organizing strategy to break that down. Because it's certainly not a very hopeful thing to think about.

Point 7
The New Affected White Americans

SHARON: What do the new, Whites or European Americans think now when they're thrown in, lumped into, a category of receiving services and human services from the government?

TIM: This is the challenge. The problem is when you've had four decades of demonization of any type of program for the have not's or have lessor's, those White folks who find themselves in need have got to deal with the belief that they are personally to blame. They're lazy, they made bad choices. How does the human mind deal with that sense of self-blame? This is the horrific irony of right-wing political and social and economic ideology. As long as it's working for you, it's working for you. But, the minute it doesn't work for you, you're left with self-blame because that's what you've come to believe.

You've said all along, 'get a job, get a job, if you don't have a job, get a job'. Now, all of a sudden you can't find a job, and it can be psychologically very distressing. When one is psychologically distressed, one can blame oneself. But there's a built-in defense mechanism not to let that happen, or you can blame the system and start to realize that, "Well, maybe the system isn't what I thought it was." But that's tough because everything you've been taught your whole life is that everybody can do it if they just try hard.

If you believe that you've tried harder, and you don't understand the systemic barriers, then the only other option–and it's the one I think we're seeing used more and more by some of these White folks who are struggling right now–is to project outward. To deflect the blame, to project it onto others. We'll project it onto immigrants. Well, if we could just close the border, our taxes would go down and we would have a job. If we could just get rid of affirmative action, if we could just get rid of this program or that program, then all of a sudden everything will be better.

I think unfortunately, that's where a lot of White Americans are falling. Instead of actually making them rethink scapegoating, it's making them go further towards it. I do think it provides us an opening to have that honest conversation about the system.

Bottom line, you can blame immigrants, you can blame welfare, you can blame affirmative action. You can do all that, but at some point you have to come clean with the facts. And the reality is an economic system that was never intended to benefit the vast majority of people in this country, including the vast majority of White folks. We just had the luxury for generations of thinking that this system was set up for us.

While we certainly had it better than People of Color, the top one half of one percent, really couldn't care less about the fundamental well-being of the vast majority of the rest of us. They think that when we don't have the ability to pay our mortgage because we got roped into a predatory loan, that we're the ones to blame.

A lot of those who lost were really hardworking middle-class families who had gotten lied to by banks. They too, had been lied to by lenders, they'd been lied to by independent mortgage brokers who got them into loans saying, "Oh, don't worry, the interest rate, yeah, in three years it's going to go up, but don't worry, we'll renegotiate it." Then of course, they didn't, and the lenders were making money hand over fist. They were deceiving the borrowers.

Then, when the borrowers lost their shirt, these folks who speak for the top one half of one percent or the top one-tenth of one percent laughed at the rest of us. That's what this is about. And the quicker that millions of working class White folks figure that out–that they're being gamed by the same system that for years was gaming Black and Brown folks– the better off we're going to be.

Point 8
Do Black and Brown People Believe the Lie?

SHARON: It isn't just solely Whites or European Americans. There are People of Color who actually believe this lie, or distortion of reality.

TIM: Sure, and of course People of Color who believe this lie will be propelled to the forefront of the conservative movement. Because that's a movement that desperately needs Black and Brown faces to give cover to their own ideology. You go to a Tea Party and there's some Black people around, you can bet they're going to be on camera. You can bet not only are they going to be on camera, they're going to be on stage. They're going to be front and center, very prominent, because it allows the right to pass itself off as something other than what it is, which is a party that for forty years has deliberately sought to push buttons of racial resentment.

What's funny is every now and then they'll admit it. Lee Atwater, who was one of the most prominent Republican consultants and campaign managers in this country's history, managed the '88 campaign for George H.W. Bush, and worked with Reagan and others. Lee Atwater died of cancer in the early '90s or mid-'90s.

When he was dying, he was talking about what he had been doing. He said 'this is what we did,' and he was ashamed of it. He had his little "come to Jesus" moment where he said we realized starting in the '70s that you couldn't just yell the N-word anymore, so we had to say it other ways. We talked about welfare, we talked about taxes, and we talked about busing. He admitted that is what he was doing. The fact that an awful lot of White folks fell for it, and that some People of Color did, is undeniable.

SHARON: *I'm familiar with that story also. I wonder how many of our listening audience members even know about that story. Because I don't think it got a lot of profile for a long period of time in any kind of healing way.*

TIM: Right, it didn't. Folks who are interested will find it's really a very telling story. Atwater was a very interesting figure, very polarizing figure, but he did have this realization late in life. Whatever, whether it was a deathbed confession or whatever it was, he had come to the conclusion that he had helped to contribute to some really fundamentally politically evil things.

There's a documentary about him actually called *Boogie Man: The Lee Atwater Story* on PBS. I don't want to imply by anything I'm saying here that all Republicans or all conservatives are motivated by racism; that's certainly not what I'm saying. I am saying that it's very hard to understand modern conservative politics the last forty years or so without understanding the centrality of race in our politics as a country.

It was possible to be a conservative without race being central, certainly. Even if everyone in the United States was the same race, we'd still have conservative people who believed in limited government or whatever. The thing is, in this country for the last forty or fifty years, that debate has been inherently connected to a debate over race, and a debate over the racial distribution of stuff. It's impossible to separate it.

If everyone in the U.S. was the same race, we'd still have conservative people who believed in limited government.

Nobody age 40 or older can say that they have come up in an era where conservatism existed separate from a racial dynamic. It just isn't true. It's not that all Republicans or that all conservatives are racist, and it's not that all liberals and Democrats aren't. There was a survey taken right before the '08 election which found that a large number of White voters for Obama still believed, according to their own admission, to a whole host of negative stereotypes about Black people. They were just making an exception for this one Black guy.

Not all Republicans are racist, and there are plenty of Democrats who I'm sure are. But that's what we've got to contend with, that all of our perceptions have been shaped by this racial framing for the last four and five decades.

Point 9
Institutionalized Racism and White People

CALLER: Marie in Missouri: *Is there a large scale way to teach White people that this is a nation of institutionalized racism, and we really don't have a level playing field?*

TIM: There's no silver bullet. It's one of the things that my work is principally focused on trying to make that case to White folks for understanding where we are now and also figuring out where we need to go. No, there's certainly no silver bullet. If there were, I wouldn't have to keep doing it, and other thousands of us who do this work, other White folks and People of Color could all take a break and not have to do it. I think that if we have the conversation where we talk about our own experiences connected to institutions, that's the best chance we have. I think sometimes we try to make this argument. We make it in an overly academic, intellectual way.

Like I said before, the sad thing is, research says numbers don't matter, facts don't matter. People who are really bought into a particular world view dig in harder when you give them facts that contradict their world view. What's interesting in my experience is that if I tell stories that demonstrate institutional racism, and maybe only after telling the story link it to some data or research, it has a bigger impact. That's why my first book, *White Like Me*, was a memoir rather than a fact-based, heavily footnoted volume.

I felt like if I told stories about my own life, demonstrating my own experiences with White racial privilege and institutional racism, that it would make those numbers that you might see in an academic article or in a book more real to people. Over the course of the years since that book was first published, which was in late '04, early '05, that has been my experience.

There are people who said, "Look, I read lots of books on race, but until I heard these personal stories it didn't connect for me." People will sometimes write to me and thank me for one of the other books that has a lot of footnotes and say "Oh, I really like that book. It helped me with my research paper, it helped me with my dissertation". I'll always say "thanks, I'm glad it helped you."

People will call or write or whatever and say, about *White Like Me,* that it really changed their view about thinking about race. I think if we can use our own experience and say, "Hey, it's not just that I'm telling you institutional racism is real. Here's how I know because I've seen it in action. Here's my personal story."

Yes, people can still dismiss it. Basic common decency and courtesy leads most people to be less demonstrative when they're responding to your personal narrative than if you're just giving them numbers. If you tell them about a study, they can just dismiss it without seeming to attack you. If you tell them this is what I saw in public housing and this is what I saw in the school systems that I attended, and this is what I see now with my own kids, people might not agree with you.

But, they're more inclined to at least listen, because it's personal, and they don't want to personally attack you. I think maybe that, as a strategy, starting with the personal and moving into the institutional, as sort of a one-two punch thing probably is the best approach.

Point 10
Not Everyone Likes the Racial Healing Approach

SHARON: Some people think that racial healing, even the phrasing of it, is just really soft. This isn't a surprise to you. There seem to be a number of people who consider you a lightning rod, and actually I think fear you in a way. How do you reconcile this?

TIM: I don't know if people are particularly afraid of me. I'm five-foot nine on a good day and not particularly rough. People are afraid of hearing truths spoken in an unvarnished way. There are lots of truth tellers out there on these issues, most of whom of course are People of Color.

I think what people are afraid of is just hearing unvarnished truth, because for so long, we have played games. Our politicians play games. Everything is about how can I say this in a way that's going to be best for the polls? How can I say this in a way that is going to be politically acceptable to people and not get me in trouble with a particular constituency?

I'm lucky to be an activist and a writer who doesn't really have to think about that a lot. It also helps to be a White male who has the luxury of frankly mouthing off about racism and being viewed far differently than a person of Color who speaks in the same way. You can listen to my talks online and read my articles and books, and I speak with a forcefulness that is easier for me. Not because I'm a better speaker or better writer, it's because being a White male, my threshold of acceptable anger is a lot higher.

I'm given a pass that People of Color are not, and I want to point that out, because People of Color know that's true. I want White folks to know that's true. It's not that I'm more passionate, it's not that. God knows I'm not angrier than People of Color about White supremacy and racism. I have the luxury of coming across a bit angrier perhaps and still getting away with it. I'm going to use that privilege if I have it, because if it helps, then it's worth deploying. As I deploy it, I want to make sure people understand that folks of Color, unfortunately are not given the same benefit of the doubt when they are angry.

In fact, if a person of Color expresses anger about racism, they're seen as threatening in ways that I've never, ever seen. As far as the notion of racial healing, I've gone all around the block on this and I'm still not settled on how I feel about the phraseology. Sometimes I feel like it sounds weak, but then there are other times I realize this thing has done stuff to us, it has done very personal stuff to us, and it has damaged us beyond belief, White and of Color.

Healing is part of it. I don't ever want to overdraw the illness or the sickness analogies by bringing up a word like, healing. But at the same time, I don't want to dismiss them. What I've learned is we cannot stay in our heads the whole time about this topic. It can't just be about numbers and statistics and data. I have memorized reams of data. I know virtually every study that's been done on these subjects, and I will talk about those in those moments when I think it's appropriate. If we can't talk also about what this thing does to us, what it does to our children, what it does to the future of the country from a much more affective and personal and emotional place, then no one is going to go to the barricades to change the system just because they read a good study.

Nobody is going to go to the barricades to change this system, just because they read a position paper from some non-profit organization and they see that the data actually says, "Oh my gosh, everything that I've always thought was wrong." That's not what leads society to change.

What leads them to change societies is a deep and abiding sense that if they do not make a shift and do not make a transition, that they themselves and their children and the future of their society is going to be in jeopardy. If healing sounds weak to people, let's keep in mind that very little institutional transformation is going to come about from broken people. It's very hard for people that are broken and damaged to lead a "revolution" of any type. We do have to work on ourselves even as we're working on changing the structures of the society.

Point 11
Is White Privilege Mostly about Money?

CALLER: Ron from Dallas, Texas: *Why is the concept, "White privilege" so difficult for the average White person to understand and acknowledge?*

TIM: I think that one's pretty simple. I think the reason it's hard is that we have a very skewed understanding of what privilege means. If you ask most people what does it mean to be privileged, they're thinking that it means born with a silver spoon in your mouth, having a lot of money.

If you're White and you don't have a lot of money– which most White folks are not wealthy, most White folks are decidedly middle class and working class just like everyone else– it's really easy then for a White person to say what do you mean? I'm not privileged, I don't have money, I wasn't born with money, I didn't inherit wealth.

What we need to remember is privilege is not just about money. That's a part of it, there's a material part of it for sure, and it is true that on balance White folks have generally had far better material position than People of Color. But when I talk about White privilege, I'm very deliberate about not focusing on the money part of it until after we deal with the first part, which is the psychological part.

It's the part that I try to explain. It's the ability of those of us who are White to go through our day not having to really think about our racial identity as a possible marker of negativity in a given day. We're not worried that our race is going to mark us negatively in the eyes of others and the eyes of authority figures. It's that ability to have one less thing to have to think about today. In a competitive society, having one less thing to worry about is a big deal, and it has material consequence.

I try to analogize it, and I find this to be pretty effective. I analogize it to able-bodied people. Obviously, if you're disabled you face discrimination, you face obstacles, barriers, on the basis of your identity as a person with a disability. We all know that. Those of us that are able bodied know that we can go through the day not really having to think about how I'm going to get in a building, out of a building if there's a fire at work, how do I get out? Those are the things that able-bodied people don't think about. People with disabilities who face obstacles on the basis of that identity think about that stuff regularly.

Now, that doesn't mean that those of us who are able bodied live easy lives. Lots of able-bodied people are poor, lots of able-bodied people are struggling. I don't think anybody would deny that it means on balance to be able bodied gives you access. It does give you a certain privilege, a certain advantage psychologically and maybe even materially, over people who are disabled.

The fact that there are some disabled people who are rich and some able-bodied people who are poor, would never lead someone to say, "Well, see, that just proves there's no able bodied privilege, because I know a guy who's in a wheelchair, but he's got a million dollars in the bank." What does that mean? That doesn't mean anything. It doesn't take away from the fact of able-bodied privilege, and the same is true here.

Are there White folks who are struggling? Yes, but all it means is that on balance, to be White in a society where Whiteness has been a marker of domination is to give you a leg up, so to speak. It doesn't mean that White folks will win every competition against People of Color, that they'll get every job, but it does mean that on balance to be White, just like being male, just like being rich, just like being able bodied, etc., gives you a certain advantage and it can't be ignored.

Point 12
The Holocaust and American Slavery

CALLER: Ron from Dallas, Texas: *Jewish people have been successful at making some countries and their citizens, including the United States, take ownership for allowing the Holocaust to happen. Why is it that White America feels no such obligation when it comes to slavery and its after effects?*

TIM: I think part of it is that in the last fifty years in this country, those of us who are Jewish, and I am Jewish religiously in terms of my family heritage, have been able to "become White" in a way. There was certainly a time when Jewish folks were not considered part of the White race, just like Irish folks weren't, and Italian folks weren't. In the last half of the Twentieth Century that really started to change.

Jewish folks are seen, for reasons that are complicated, as being just another type of White person. Whenever a group that is now considered White presses a claim for justice it's a lot easier for other White folks to listen to than it is when a Person of Color does. It's also easier in the case of Jewish folks who've received some sympathy for the European Holocaust. And in the case of Germany getting recompense for what hap-

> It's the ability of those of us who are White to go through our day not having to really think about our racial identity as a possible marker of negativity in a given day.

pened somewhere else. In the United States it's no sweat off our back to acknowledge it, it's no sweat off our back to talk about what Germany did.

In fact, it's interesting. Several years ago there was an adult education program for people getting their GED here in Tennessee where I live. It made the news, it was a program on tolerance they were teaching these adult education students. The curriculum was entirely about the Holocaust of European Jews. I thought, "You know, I get it."

I guess there are definitely some lessons to learn about tolerance from that historical experience. But, it struck me as very odd that they would make that the subject when I live in the city where this program on tolerance was created, in downtown Nashville, is about twenty-minutes' drive from Andrew Jackson's house.

They could have easily made a lesson about tolerance and talked about the Trail of Tears and talked about Indian removal and talked about enslavement of African peoples, but it was easier to say, "Look at those horrible people in that other country sixty years ago and what they did," than to look at what goes on in your own country–not only sixty years ago or one hundred and sixty years ago– but six minutes ago.

I think it's always easier for any country to look at the evil that others do. Let me put it this way. Had that happened to Jews in the United States, I'm not convinced that non-Jewish White folks in the United States would have been all that quick to take it seriously, in spite of the way that Jewish folks have "become White," I still think had it happened here, we would still be far less likely to honestly assess it.

Because it happened somewhere else, we can look at it and say, "Wasn't that terrible? Even though in many ways we have done exactly that to indigenous people and with regard to people of African descent.

Point 13
Our Future

SHARON: Do you think our future is very bright and hopeful, or do you think that our future is fraught with a lot of contention about this subject?

TIM: I'm going to say that it's both of those things. I think we're in for some very difficult days, and I think we're in for several years of real soul searching and very difficult conflict around issues of race as this country becomes a 50/50, People of Color/White country.

I do think however, that people have the capacity to create justice. I have to say I'm agnostic on it because I haven't seen it yet, but I believe that it's possible and I know one thing. We're only on this earth for a very short period of time. In that period, I can't think of a much better purpose to put one's life to use than the purpose of creating justice.

Whether it can happen or whether it can't, what are our options? You either do the work or you don't. If you don't, you know you won't have justice. If you do the work perhaps you will, so let's just leave it at that.

Interview Summary

The range of Tim's knowledge and clear insights into the why and how, have made this one of the most talked about interviews. Tim Wise takes us on a journey of personal discovery punctuated with a level of truth telling about ourselves, our country, and our institutions not commonly heard from a White male. Is there something about the New Orleans and Southern experience in his background that plants seeks to seek out justice? The old saying that, the South will lead the way on racial justice before the North, comes to mind.

The psychology of White imagination, when White people need to use safety nets, when some Black people gain a stage in Tea Party politics, when White people figure out the lie...when...when...when. As a White male, Tim knows full well that he can constructively use his White privilege to say what many People of Color are also saying without much penalty. Tim accurately says that if a Black person said what he says, there would be more fear and dismissal.

He shows how White people are affected by racism as well, but may not connect the dots as readily. I refer to it as White people thinking People of Color are whining about race. I'd like to hear what Tim thinks in the next ten to fifteen years. It's bound to be as enlightening and instrumental in moving forward.

Points for Discussion

1) What is your White or People of Color imagination about race? Can you tell or list your trail or sequence of beliefs?

2) Why are we, as humans, affected more by stories than facts and statistics? Is trust a factor? Is too much data and little information another factor?

3) Tim Wise and Mayor Mitch Landrieu have New Orleans' experiences, are White, straight males with a courageous national voice on race. Are similar White voices in your region?

Reader's Notes

Interview 10

The Descendents:

Plessy AND Ferguson

When I was attending elementary school, my teachers would recognize me by my last name. Then when they were discussing the Plessy v. Ferguson case, they would often use me as an example, and stand me in front of the room and say,
"This gentleman's name is Plessy."

Keith Plessy-Descendent of Homer Plessy

I got a phone call from the current occupant of Judge John Ferguson's house, who had been trying to track me down for information about the house. In the course of that conversation, he talked about the judge, my great-great-grandfather, and wondered if I had any information on this house. I actually didn't know that I was related to Judge Ferguson until that moment! It was kind of a shock.

Phoebe Ferguson-Descendent of Judge John Ferguson

Keith Plessy

Phoebe Ferguson

PLESSY AND FERGUSON

Keith M. Plessy is a bellman at The Marriott hotel. He graduated from the New Orleans Center for Creative Arts. The gifted artist has painted hundreds of Civil Rights portraits. As the president of the Plessy Ferguson Foundation, Keith tirelessly reaches out to the community.

Phoebe Ferguson returned to her native home of New Orleans after graduating from New York University to make *Member of the Club,* a film about the rise of New Orleans' Black middle class. She works at the Foundation and shares the importance of documenting stories, the past and legacy.

Keith Weldon Medley is author of *We as Freemen – Plessy v. Ferguson,* and is a recipient of Louisiana Endowment for the Humanities. His publications include *Smithsonian* magazine, *The Times-Picayune* and *Southern Exposure.*

Brenda Billips Square specializes in African-American history, race relations and is an archivist and librarian. She collected oral histories after Hurricane Katrina and received a Peace award.

The founders of The Plessy and Ferguson Foundation all are natives of New Orleans.

Keith Weldon Medley   Brenda Billips Square

THE DIALOGUE

I'm always reminded that, that long arc of racial healing can take a very long time. But how sweet the voices of the descendants who correct injustices! Before the courageous act of Rosa Parks on a public bus system in 1955, Homer Plessy refused to move from a seat on a train in 1892.

His courageous act of civil disobedience sparked the U.S. Supreme Court decision to uphold separate-but-equal laws. Judge John Ferguson won his case. *Plessy v. Ferguson* set in motion another low point in our history. But, where are some of the descendants of *Plessy v. Ferguson* today? What would happen if they actually met? We now know they are chartering a new legacy of racial healing, and have not let past ancestors seal their separate ways.

Every school teaches about *Plessy v. Ferguson*. But, the history books seem to stop at the chapter about being against one another. There is a new history being written in front of our eyes. The descendants Keith Plessy and Phoebe Ferguson will share an important peek inside the moving story of how a bad stretch of history has not stopped their ability to create and live a new legacy through healing and community action. As usual, it takes a village along with Keith W. Medley, acclaimed author of *We as Freemen*, and archivist Brenda Billips Square.

POINT 1
What Happened?
Was This Planned or Accident?

MEDLEY: *Plessy v. Ferguson* is one of the most famous, or infamous, Supreme Court cases having to do with race relations. Homer Plessy was a shoemaker in New Orleans. In 1890, Louisiana passed a law that forced Blacks and Whites to be separated on the railroad trains.

The next year, eighteen people got together to have this law overturned by the courts. They were going to do this by raising money and bringing awareness to what was going on. In 1892, Homer Adolph Plessy presented himself to be arrested so that they could have a test case to bring before the court. That's how *Plessy v. Ferguson* got started. It was by design. Plessy was sort of a Rosa Parks of the 1890s.

I was born during the "separate but equal," era, and my parents lived mostly their whole lives through it. Personally, it has a real effect on my life.

SHARON: *Was Homer Plessy an identifiable, if you will, person of African descent? Would someone notice him and obviously see that he was African American?*

MEDLEY: Actually, no, he wasn't. He was very light-skinned. He could pass for White. One of the reasons they did that was so he would be able to get on the train without being molested, because they wanted to present this as a test case. That's just another example of how it takes all of us to participate in the struggle for freedom and liberty and unity in our country. How long did "Separate but Equal" stay in effect before it was overturned?

The decision came in 1896, and it was set aside by *Brown v. Board* of

Education in 1954. It was at least a half a century. I was born during Separate but Equal, and my parents lived mostly their whole lives through it. Personally, it has a real effect on my life, and many other people.

SHARON: Your book, We As Freemen: Plessy v. Ferguson, is one that really has a lot of great accolades associated with it. I would encourage anyone and everyone out there to go take a look, buy a book, and really read this detailed history about Plessy v. Ferguson and what really happened. Keith Medley, is there a picture of Homer Plessy available?

MEDLEY: People have said that they have seen a picture of Homer Plessy, but there is none available that I know of. There are images of him that people say are him on websites but they're really not.

POINT 2
Today: Keith Plessy and Phoebe Ferguson

SHARON: Now we can take a look and introduce some of the descendants as Plessy AND Ferguson. I really enjoy saying it that way, too. Keith Plessy, tell us a little bit about how it came that you knew about your famous history.

PLESSY: I can go back as far as my elementary school years, when I attended the Lancey Jones School in New Orleans. The teachers were very good teachers. They went beyond the book. As many people know, all we have in our history books about *Plessy v. Ferguson* is about a paragraph. It does not explain what the case was about, and it does not go into the intricacies that Keith Medley's book goes into, when researching all of the characters involved in that case.

When I was attending elementary school, my teachers would recognize me by my last name. Then when they were discussing the *Plessy v.*

Ferguson case, they would often use me as an example, and stand me in front of the room, and say, "This gentleman's name is Plessy."

They would talk about the case, and go in more detail, for whatever information they had to share. It was then that I realized that I was related to him, because we would look in the phone books, and we would see that there were very few Plessy's in New Orleans, there had to be some connection.

In my junior and senior high school years, the same paragraph existed in the history books. It didn't explain much more about Homer Plessy. It wasn't until 1996, that I learned much more about my relationship to Homer Plessy when family genealogy research was done. In 1996, Keith Medley was deep into his research about his book, and I met him at a conference in New Orleans called, "When the Future was the Past." It was celebrating the 100th anniversary of the *Plessy v. Ferguson* decision. It took place here in New Orleans, and several universities around the country participated.

We had a mock funeral to commemorate Homer Plessy and bury him as free man, because in his time, we considered that he may have had the impression that he died in a time that he would never see freedom. *Separate but Equal* was the law of the land in 1926 when he passed away. With Keith Medley's research, and just becoming a good friend of Keith Weldon Medley at that time, we constantly stayed in touch with each other, and he shared a wealth of information with me.

When his book was published in 2003, I met one of my relatives from two hundred years removed. Originally, there were two Plessys who came to the United States: Jermaine and Dominique. Jermaine was my and Homer Plessy's line; Dominique moved to Lake George Parish. The gentleman who helped Keith Medley work on his book was Bobby Duplessy, and he helped him do the genealogy research on Homer Plessy. He asked to meet a Plessy who lived in New Orleans, and Keith happened to know me, so he introduced us.

In 2003, I met my relative who was separated from the two brothers who separated for about 200 years. They arrived in the early 1800s, in the United States. Keith's book was the key to everything, as far as this foundation is concerned, as well, because through his book in 2004, a year later I met Phoebe Ferguson.

SHARON: Phoebe Ferguson, can you tell us a little bit about your history and story?

FERGUSON: I was born and raised in New Orleans. I didn't actually know that I was related to the same Judge Ferguson until 2002. By that time I was living in Brooklyn. I got a phone call from the current occupant of Judge Ferguson's house, who had been trying to track me down for information about the house. In the course of that conversation, he talked about the judge, my great-great-grandfather, and wondered if I had any information on this house. I actually didn't know that I was related to Judge Ferguson until that moment! It was kind of a shock.

Interestingly enough, just about a week before I had received a genealogy diagram, and I quickly went to that diagram, looked back, and there he was, Judge John Howard Ferguson, from Martha's Vineyard. That's what started my journey. Very quickly, I too discovered Keith Medley and his book, and came to New Orleans and met him. And it was through Keith Medley that I met Keith Plessy in 2004.

SHARON: These are prime examples about how we feel in the healing of racism, that we're born into these stories and we don't know the others' parts and pieces. Now, you two lived in the same city, or grew up in the same city, New Orleans, and had no clue, no idea, in earlier years, really, about how you were related to one of the most famous or infamous cases in U.S. history. How did you feel when you found that out?

FERGUSON: I just will say, I think that neither of us had any idea how it was going to change our lives. I would certainly say, in that moment, you could feel that something was definitely happening, and that Keith and I had a connection from the beginning, I think.

SHARON: *How about you, Keith? How did that feel, when you realized who some of your ancestors were?*

PLESSY: It was a great awakening for me. What it did for me was open a door to where my daughters would never guess, like I didn't, about my history, about our ancestors' history. That just a wealth of information began to come out. There's more information that came out afterwards–going into Homer Plessy's ancestors–that was very surprising.

Homer Plessy's great-grandmother was a lady by the name of Agnes Matthieu, who purchased her freedom. She was a slave. She purchased her freedom in 1779. She fought in Spanish court for her freedom for about a year, because that's how long the trial went on. Four generations later, Homer Plessy fights for his freedom in U.S. Supreme Court, and four generations later, here I am. I'm blessed to found this Foundation with Phoebe Ferguson.

POINT 3
The First Meeting of Phoebe and Keith

SHARON: *Phoebe, what was it like when you two first met? I can't imagine.*

FERGUSON: The actual moment was pretty great. We came into this building called the Preservation Resource Center, where Keith Medley was going to give a talk about his book, because it had just recently been published. Since he knew Keith Plessy already, he had arranged for Keith to be there.

We walked in, and Keith Medley looked and me, and he said, "Phoebe Ferguson, I want you to meet somebody." Keith Plessy walked up with a big smile on his face, and he said, "Hi, I'm Keith Plessy."

I said, "I'm Phoebe Ferguson." Then suddenly, it just sort of . . . I said, "Oh, I'm so sorry." Like, oh, my God, you know? All of a sudden, the whole history was in my lap. It just, I didn't expect it to come out. Then Keith just looked at me, and he said, "Phoebe Ferguson, it's OK. It's no longer *Plessy v. Ferguson*. It's Plessy **AND** Ferguson." That was in 2004 when it became Plessy AND Ferguson.

PLESSY: I think Phoebe Ferguson summed it all up. I had no idea, when I said, "It's no longer *Plessy VS. Ferguson*, it's Plessy **AND** Ferguson," that we would actually form a foundation named "Plessy and Ferguson Foundation." Those words came straight from my heart, and I meant those words.

And we, shortly after, just developed a friendship that continued through the worst hours in our lifetime, which we consider to be Hurricane Katrina, which came a little bit after 2004, right in 2005. Our friendship just blossomed throughout the disaster. Phoebe Ferguson's documentary film, "Member of the Club," was in the process of verifying their story, and after Katrina hit, they had nothing.

SHARON: Member of the Club, is a film about the rise of New Orleans' Black middle class. I know this is a little bit of an aside, but this film was before you met Keith Plessy, or after?

FERGUSON: I started it just about the time I found out. I started just before I found out about my relationship to the Judge. I started filming in 2003, and I finished in 2005; we met in the middle of it.

Actually, there's a section in the film with Keith Plessy. Both Keith Medley and Keith Plessy are in the film. The film gives the history of New Orleans from about 1895 to 2005. How it parallels sort of – New Orleans' White upper class and the rise of New Orleans' Black upper class – and the struggles during that time to have equal opportunity, socially, educationally, and on all levels.

That just happened. It just made the film so rich, to be able to include them.

POINT 4
Emotionally Dealing with the History

SHARON: That is just a remarkable sequence of events. I wanted to also get back to a point, Phoebe, where you mentioned that when you first met Keith Plessy, you said, "I'm sorry." Where did that come from? Did that take courage for you to even come to that meeting? Tell us a little bit about that.

FERGUSON: I'm really glad you asked that, because it really is a struggle. I mean, I'll be really honest with you. It's hard. It's really hard to be, like, on my side of the history, in a way, because I have to ask myself, "Well, how do I deal with this?" "What am I responsible for?" You know? And, "What does the legacy of my name mean? How do I approach it?"

I always think that if I hadn't met Keith, what would I do with that information? I think it would just be there as a piece of family history I wish I didn't have to admit. I wouldn't have anything to work with it. I would just kind of say, you know, "I wish people didn't ask me this," you know, or something. With Keith, I have a way to work with history, and a legacy, and talk, and actually talk about it out loud.

SHARON: As a part of the Human race and the White "race," we have to look at this history, and we have to try to understand why we made these choices, and how we're going to move forward in a more positive way. I'm hoping that this meeting of you two was very much liberating. In the healing of racism, the work that we do, and why we do this show, we share that our histories are really not our fault.

We are truly born into these stories, and so it takes courage, especially at times, for European-Americans to literally face that history in or-

I always think that if I hadn't met Keith what would I do with that information? I think it would just be there as a piece of family history I wish I didn't have to admit.

der to move forward. Keith, your book seems to be a pivot point in basically the turning of history with the meeting of Keith Plessy and Phoebe Ferguson. Tell us a little bit about how that feels; to be kind of like the engineer, here?

MEDLEY: It's been a very gratifying sojourn, for me. I've been researching Plessy since the 1980s. It was strange, because he lived right around my house, where I grew up, but there was so little about him in New Orleans that was public. I had no idea that this big Civil Rights Movement happened in my neighborhood. That was very interesting.

The other gratifying thing was that not only did I write the book about it, but the fact that my book was able to bring together a family that has been separated by race for two hundred years– I'm talking about Bobby Duplessy, and that Keith and Phoebe Ferguson have been able to take this gauntlet upon themselves. I think their message is, if Plessy *AND* Ferguson can come together after one hundred years, well, there's hope for us all. I mean, this was the case that defined *Separate but Equal*, and now Keith and Phoebe Ferguson here, are flipping the script on it, and now it stands for racial understanding and racial reconciliation.

POINT 5
Archiving and Preserving for Our Future

SHARON: Brenda Square, you had an instrumental role in the unfolding of this story too, as an archivist and librarian. Can you tell us a little bit about why you do what you do?

SQUARE: Being a librarian and an archivist, we have a huge gap in written records which detail our history of race relations and civil rights in America. We see this especially in New Orleans' role in shaping American race relations. I knew Keith Medley for many years frankly, and as a researcher in the archives, watched his work and research. Then, I met Keith Plessy. We've all really been interested and involved in community work.

In 1996, I was at the Amistad Research Center, and we had a huge event to commemorate the *Plessy v. Ferguson* decision. Medley did a wonderful exhibition and Plessy and I were on a documentary together. Then, here comes Phoebe Ferguson in the archives! I'd had an opportunity to work with her doing research on her film, *Member of the Club*.
We got to know each other, and I began to see that it was not a coincidence that these people were coming together at this time in American history.

I didn't think it was a coincidence that we were all kind of united in our interest in education and racial healing. We were kind of figuring out what we could do. All the time, in many, many lunches, and discussions, and meetings, we were just led to believe that we had to make this a permanent kind of organization. We didn't know how to do it, and I really struggled with the name. Watching Keith Plessy and Phoebe Ferguson together, I knew that this was his story.

Archivists are trained to recognize historic documents, records, events, which are important for preservation and which will be important for the future. I recognized that having Keith Plessy and Phoebe Ferguson working together was unique in American history. We could use their involvement to help spread racial understanding and awareness, and the importance of the case.

Medley had done this great book, and it was pivotal in shaping this development. I knew that God had his hand on us in all of this. I have been here, as the archivist, just trying to help develop our Sacred Spaces project in New Orleans, about marking historic sites post-Katrina. We're very concerned, because, as Keith Medley said, he grew up in this neighborhood not realizing, not understanding that all these major events occurred right where he walked every day. And when he discovered this, it changed his whole life.

We want to do this for the children in our city and our nation. We want them to understand the role of our state, and how it has impacted and shaped American history. We have Plessy and Ferguson with us now, and we want America to meet them, and to see what our history has been. We look for fun, creative, and interesting ways to present the story.

POINT 6
Writing the New History

SHARON: This is writing history as we speak– the new history of Plessy and Ferguson. You have a foundation now, The Plessy and Ferguson Foundation. What is the Foundation about, what is your mission, and what are you looking to do?

PLESSY: Our original mission was to create a new and innovative way to teach the history of Civil Rights through understanding of the case and its effect on the American conscience. Since then, we have improved the mission statement to fostering understanding between all races by helping our communities establish fruitful connections to the past. We do this through education, preservation, and outreach.

Through each program, we've been working with education. We announced the Foundation on the property where the New Orleans Center for Creative Arts (NOCA) is located. The NOCA is one of our major partners since we began. That's at the corner of Press and Royal Streets, where our original marker for the *Plessy v. Ferguson* case is set-up. That was the site where Homer Plessy was arrested.

We've worked with NOCA in creating what we have as a holiday called Plessy Day. Every June 7, we commemorate the arrest of Homer Plessy. It took place June 7, 1892 on that corner of Press and Royal Street where the plaque is. In 2009 we coordinated with NOCA on the dance group for the summer, coordinated the appeal, so we combined history and dance on that particular holiday.

In 2010, the next year, we had a play that was developed by NOCA's drama division. It was called *Separate*. This play is an evolving play that has the students act out roles as themselves, and they relate to Keith's book. The characters show how segregation all the way from 1892, 1896, until now affects them in their lives. The roles constantly change. As the students graduate, they'll have a new student come up and take over that role the next year.

FERGUSON: All of us are very concerned with education, on many levels. Historically and certainly today, we have a new landscape with the reform movement in public education. We do a lot of research on that end. In terms of teaching legacy, and maybe through my own work with documentary film, it gives us an opportunity to meld the arts and to have individual students figure out what their story is, and their family relationships to history and where they live. And then use film as a medium to tell that story, and to interview their relatives, and people in their neighborhood, and try to put the pieces together to figure out who they are.

That's one element to that. Brenda Square can talk about this, too, but she's very involved in working on new curriculums in education and how we can make the case actually sort of a core curriculum to Civil Rights history. This is the new history. What comes to mind immediately, for me, is that if history books today have still a paragraph about *Plessy v. Ferguson*, and they're not updated to tell about Plessy AND Ferguson, how much of an educational loss is that?

SQUARE: That is why we embrace outreach as a part of our initial mission, by looking for creative and innovative ways to bridge history. We don't have the time to wait for the scholars to come into the archives and do a dissertation and write articles before this material will get into the textbooks.

We are becoming activists, archivists, historians, and community, to bring the history to the classrooms, and partner with teachers. We're looking now to find ways to partner with educators and write curriculums to tell the story of Keith Plessy and Phoebe Ferguson, and Medley's book. To use these resources, these primary sources, the stories of Keith Plessy and Phoebe Ferguson's families, as well as the rich material that Keith Medley has preserved in his book, those secondary sources, to bring that to the classroom today.

The play *Separate,* done at the NOCA, is an example of how we are combining the arts to teach history. We want to do math. We want to embrace science. We want to find and partner with educators so that they will understand that in order for our nation to move forward, for real racial healing to take place, we need a serious commitment to teach the full story of our nation's history.

We can do it in a way that will be positive and uplifting. No one should hold their heads down. This is our past, and if we want to move forward, we must acknowledge it, embrace it, and learn from it, so that we don't repeat the same mistakes.

Today, we have new legislation being enacted which looks very similar to the old voting rights laws which kept people from voting many years ago. And legislators vote on these things because they don't know history.

We have made a serious commitment to take Phoebe Ferguson and Keith Plessy on the road, and Keith Medley with his book. We want to tell the stories, and to plant seeds to grow future historians, archivists, and preservationists, so we can make a Civil Rights trail in our city marking where Plessy and his community–the Citizen's Committee– worked.

Then we're going throughout that community, installing plaques in what we call our Sacred Spaces. Spaces that we want marked forever, where people will be able to go and look and understand the true history of our community and its involvement in shaping the American story.

Now we know what happened with the family stories; the genealogists have done the work. The partnering with the genealogists, historians, archivists and public school teachers will make a difference for the future.

I feel compelled, that we must do that. Now we know what happened with the family stories; the genealogists have done the work. Partnering with the genealogists, historians, archivists and public school teachers will make a difference for the future.

POINT 7
The Future of the Foundation

SHARON: The foundation is looking to do a lot more outreach. Can you tell us a little bit about outreach, and what that means to the Foundation?

MEDLEY: I think outreach is very important. Just from my perspective, it's, like, Homer Plessy has evolved over the years. First he was a shoemaker, then, he was an arrestee. For the long part of Homer Plessy's life, he was just a court case, without any humanity attached to it.

I think that the work that we have been doing, around New Orleans, is so that many more people will know that this was a part of the Civil Rights Movement. We've put up two plaques. And so, we have been going around sowing our seeds to get this information out. I think it's been working. When I look at how people used to look at this case, and how they do now, they realize that it was part of the Civil Rights Movement.

FERGUSON: I would say that my office is about a block from the Homer Plessy plaque, the *Plessy v. Ferguson* plaque, and you really have no idea how invigorating it is to walk by and see people standing there, reading the plaque. There was nothing there before, and now they're absolutely engrossed in this.

Imagining history at that location, and then connecting the dots. That form of outreach is permanent and will be there for people to constantly make this connection for themselves about this historic site.

SQUARE: I'd like to put up more plaques. We have a list of sites that we have decided we want to permanently mark, and preserve the significance of these sites, so that people, when they come to the city, will know about the events of our history, which occurred on those sites. We hope to do one a year, and we've put together a nice partnership with the state. We know how to get approval for the markers. We want to mark an area in the uptown New Orleans which was a Civil Rights corridor.

There's a public school that was very important. It was the first teacher training institution where Keith Plessy attended school, and it's also a school where he did Civil Rights murals. It's been abandoned since the storm. It's in the Seventh Ward's Lucy Jones School. We want to actually make a trail of historic sites, so that when people visit our city, they will be able to go and visit these markers, and get a new understanding of the history of our community.

At the same time, with our commitment to racial healing and truth, we want to complete the telling of our history.

POINT 8
Your Families' Reaction to This History

SHARON: When we think about Plessy and Ferguson, and the courage that it takes–especially for you, Phoebe as a European-American–to participate in this process, how are your family members taking this?

FERGUSON: Unfortunately, both my parents are not living anymore. It would have been very interesting. I will say that my mother was very liberal, and taught me well. We were raised by an African-American nanny who I loved deeply. My mother also loved her. My father's background, on the Ferguson side, you know, there was a lot of bigotry.

I remember it very well, and I remember being very upset by it, as a small child, not understanding it, and, you know, not being able to resolve it in my mind, the two ways of relating to all the people that I cared about in my life. I don't know how exactly they would respond today, but I know that there would be different backgrounds and it would be very interesting. I really wish I could see what their response would have been. I have a brother and sister, and they're very happy that we're doing this work.

SHARON: Keith, when you first met Phoebe Ferguson, you embraced her.

PLESSY: Yes, I did. My upbringing consisted of a very religious mother who raised me, and she taught me to love everyone. I can't say that I've been great at it all my life, but it just seemed as though, in this instance, I didn't really choose to become the president of the Plessy and Ferguson Foundation. In many ways, I was chosen. I feel like it's divine work that we're taking part in. We're doing the work of the Father. All this work will come out well.

I'm learning, as we know each other more, because when I first met Phoebe Ferguson there were no bad vibes in the room. She was a good person. I could tell from the first comment she made. We've just been good friends throughout our relationship. And I thought, in the beginning, that we just could become friends, just from a simple friendship. I had no idea that it would become a movement like this. And it has become a movement.

FERGUSON: We have a Facebook page! We all still have other jobs that we do in addition to the Foundation work. We could always use volunteer help to spread the word, and be on committees, get those plaques up, and help us with curriculums. We are very open to having people help us with the work.

POINT 9
Biggest Surprise

SHARON: What has been the biggest surprise for you on this journey?

PLESSY: I met Keith Medley in 1996. In 1997, I met Rosa Parks at my hotel. If I had any doubts in my mind as to what I was going to do–and I did–that cleared it up for me after that meeting.

FERGUSON: I think the biggest surprise is that my life has taken such an interesting turn, and that I have the opportunity to work with Keith Plessy, Keith Medley, and Brenda Square and actually to have a voice out there in the world on Civil Rights and our future.

Interview Summary

If your eyes aren't wet with being a witness to this currently unfolding history, I don't know what to say. Keith Plessy and Phoebe Ferguson have walked into making a new history that we can be very proud of. It wouldn't have happened without Keith Medley's unstoppable curiosity and passion, or Brenda Square's dedication to archiving.

Now, we stand another shining chance to tell the new story with a middle part in full public view. The ending will be when all of the story is available for everyone to be educated about so that there will be little chance of the awful part of our history remaining a terrible legacy.

Who would have thought the legacy of *Plessy v. Ferguson* would be so rich with promise and have an ending we all can share? Someone, please get the movie script ready!

Points for Discussion

1) Did you know *Plessy v. Ferguson* began in New Orleans? When did you first hear about this historic case?

2) This part of history took more than one hundred years to go from separate, to equal accommodations. What legacy are you committed to in the next twenty-five years?

3) Both Keith Plessy and Phoebe Ferguson chose to build this new legacy. What is it about their background and life experience that set the stage to be welcoming and fearless with each other?

Reader's Notes

INTERVIEW GUEST
CONTACT
INFORMATION
&
AUTHOR

Interview Guest Contact Information

Interview 1- *Life After Hate: A Former Skinhead's Tale of Racism and Redemption*
Angela King- angelaking@lifeafterhate.org or www.lifeafterhate.org

Interview 2- *Unraveling the White Privilege Knot...not?*
Allan Johnson, Ph.D.- www.agjohnson.us/

Interview 3- *When People of Color Turn to Self Hate*
Hugh Vasquez- hvasquez@nationalequityproject.org or
www.nationalequityproject.org

Interview 4- *Psychiatrist Talks Race and Human Development*
James P. Comer, M.D.- James.Comer@yale.edu or
www.schooldevelopmentprogram.org/about/people/faculty/comer.aspx

Interview 5- *New Orleans Mayor Talks Racial Healing*
Mitchell J. Landrieu- mayor@nola.gov or www.nola.gov/mayor/

Interview 6- *Being Asian: The Reality, Triumph, and Challenge*
Evaon Wong-Kim, Ph.D. evaon@csueastbay.edu or
www20.csueastbay.edu/class/departments/socialwork/

Interview 7- *Think You Know a Lot About Arab Americans? Really?*
Charles Khalil Alawan, Hajj- muhammadlegacy@aol.com

Interview 8- *Can Sexual Orientation and Racial Healing Coexist?*
James M. Croteau, Ph.D., Acclaimed Professor- james.croteau@wmich.edu or
www.homepages.wmich.edu/~croteau/
Donna R. Payne, Human Rights Campaign Expert- donna.payne@hrc.org or
www.hrc.org/staff/profile/donna-payne

Interview 9- *Tim Wise Talks: A New Demonizing Trend?*
Tim Wise- tmjwise@mac.com www.tmwise.org

Interview 10- *The Descendants Plessy AND Ferguson*
Keith Plessy- kmplessy.1892@yahoo.com
Phoebe Ferguson- info@plessyandferguson.org
Keith Weldon Medley- kwmedley@gmail.com or www.keithweldonmedley.com
Brenda Billips Square- brenda.square@gmail.com
The Plessy and Ferguson Foundation- info@theplessyandfergusonfoundaton.org

228

SHARON E. DAVIS

Sharon is a founding member of the Institute for Healing of Racism established in 1987. She has conducted International Dialogue Racism sessions in Mmabatho, South Africa, facilitated a public seminar on Cultural and Tribal Unity in Gabaronne, Botswana and facilitated talks on conflict resolution in China.

Our author has been quoted and published in various publications as it relates to racial healing, and was interviewed by McNeil/Lehrer Newshour for the "Healing Racism in America" segment. She served as an International Institute and U.S. Immigration Services speaker, was mistress of ceremonies at swearing-in ceremonies for new Americans and a regular TV panelist on "Interfaith Odyssey." Sharon also has served as advisor and former executive director at the National Resource Center for Racial Healing, which included being a project advisor for Diversity with NASA's Jet Propulsion Laboratory Saturn Titan Mission.

The dedicated host of the radio show, *A Safe Place to Talk About Race,* has received numerous awards for helping people unite. They include: the *Spiritual Midwife of the Millennium Award for Cultural Diversity*, one of the six *Most Influential Black Women Entrepreneurs in Metro Detroit, Diversity Champion's Honor Role* with the Birmingham-Bloomfield Multiracial Community Council, Houston, Texas' *Peace Award for Intergroup Understanding,* and Western Michigan University's *Excellence in Diversity* award.

A Safe Place to Talk **ABOUT RACE** with Sharon E. Davis

Variety

WWW.SAFEPLACEONRACE.COM
Sharon@safeplaceonrace.com   888.569.5575

For more information regarding bulk orders,

speaking engagements,

or interviews with the author, visit:

www.safeplaceonrace.com

<u>Email:</u>

info@safeplaceonrace.com

<u>Phone:</u>

888-569-5575

Made in the USA
Charleston, SC
25 March 2015